Dreaming on Both Sides of the Brain

DREAMING

on Both Sides of the Brain

Discover the Secret Language of the Night

Doris E. Cohen, PhD

Foreword from bestselling author CHRISTIANE NORTHRUP, MD

HAMPTON ROADS

Cover design by Jim Warner
Cover images: Left and right hemisphere of human brain © Cozy nook /
Shutterstock; Pillow: © Alhovik / Shutterstock
Interior Design by Steve Amarillo / Urban Design LLC
Typeset in Adobe Sabon, BA Graphics Torino Modern,
House Industries Chalet Comprimé

Hampton Roads Publishing Company, Inc.
Charlottesville, VA 22906
Distributed by Red Wheel/Weiser, LLC
www.redwheelweiser.com

Sign up for our newsletter and special offers
by going to *www.redwheelweiser.com/newsletter/*.

ISBN: 978-1-57174-797-6

Library of Congress Cataloging-in-Publication Data
Names: Cohen, Doris Eliana, 1943- author.
Title: Dreaming on both sides of the brain : discover the secret language of
the night / Doris E. Cohen.
Description: Charlottesville : Hampton Roads Pub., 2017.
Identifiers: LCCN 2017010508 | ISBN 9781571747976 (6 x 9 tp : alk. paper)
Subjects: LCSH: Dreams. | Dream interpretation.
Classification: LCC BF1091 .C625 2017 | DDC 154.6/3--dc23
LC record available at https://lccn.loc.gov/2017010508

Printed in Canada
MAR
10 9 8 7 6 5 4 3 2 1

This book is dedicated to all nations, all races—to all living beings. With all my heart and soul, my wish is that, after reading this book, you will be able to understand the magic of your dreams and apply that language to your waking life so you can truly discover your path and bring enriched meaning to your existence. This book is my dream!

To all who have helped me on this amazing path of dreams, I give my profound love and appreciation.

CONTENTS

Part III: Working with Dreams

Part IV: Interpreting Your Own Dreams

Conclusion: The Power of Choice

ACKNOWLEDGMENTS

Profound thanks to Dr. Christiane Northrup, a staunch friend and colleague who has been my avid supporter and who has always given me encouragement and hope. I am deeply grateful for your invaluable help in putting my dreamwork into motion—swiftly and gracefully, and with loyalty and compassion. Your belief in me has been instrumental in making my dream come true and I thank you from the bottom of my heart.

My thanks to Nancy Shea, a very dear friend, who is creative, brilliant, and endlessly helpful. She has been my "go-to person"—a multitalented expert who has helped with everything regarding this book. And to Dr. Erika Schwartz and Debbie Barnby, both dear friends whose belief in me has never wavered.

My assistant, Robbie Myers, has been loyal and reliable, and a bulwark of strength in myriad ways that have facilitated both my work in life and in this book. Likewise, the acceptance and support of my publisher, Greg Brandenburgh, has, like Bach's concertos, been beautiful music to my ears.

And finally, my deep gratitude to Evelyn Fisboin Guttman, whose love and support has always remained shining in my life.

FOREWORD

I have been on the forefront of health and healing for decades as a pioneer in women's health. And here's what I know. To get healthy and stay healthy, you must connect with your soul—and with your unconscious, the part of you that your intellect alone can't access. Because that's where the real power lies. Dreams fall into this category. They are messages from your unconscious that report to you each and every night, loaded with information specific to you. Indeed, studies have shown that dreams can even warn of health conditions that require attention long before a dreamer is aware of them in conscious life. And no one is more qualified to guide you in how to work with your own dreams than Dr. Doris Cohen, with whom I've worked for years.

In 2012, I went to Buenos Aires for three weeks to dance the Argentine tango in the place where it originated. This dance of the heart was born in the slums and broken hearts of slaves and immigrants who came to Buenos Aires from Italy, Germany, Africa, and other places around the world. This passionate dance comes from the heart and, when practiced diligently, can often help heal it.

At the time, I was a relatively new dancer and I didn't speak Spanish. I was also a middle-aged woman recovering from a broken heart following the break-up of a relationship with a man I had been certain was *the one*. Dancing the close-embrace tango helped me heal the searing pain of loss—and satisfied a lifelong desire to learn partner dancing. So a trip to Buenos Aires was inevitable. The city and the tango music composed there called to me like a siren.

On my first day there, I was walking down a busy street enjoying the afternoon sunlight with the seasoned dancer with whom I was traveling. We had just indulged in a shopping spree and were ebullient as we basked in the first day of our tango adventure. Suddenly, I felt a pair of hands at my throat and my necklace—a very expensive gold "goddess necklace" that had been a birthday gift from a number of people who, prompted by my daughter, had all pitched in to purchase it—was snatched from my neck. I screamed. But it all happened so fast that the thief quickly crossed the crowded street and disappeared. Shaken, I was left with a bruised and scratched neck.

More than that, however, my sense of safety and happiness was shattered. I no longer felt safe or secure in that place—a place where I had planned on walking regularly in the middle of the night, to and from the tango dances known as *milongas*. When planning my trip, everyone I talked to told me how safe Buenos Aires was and that I wouldn't have to worry there. I later learned that those in the know make sure that they never wear anything valuable on the street or even take out their cell phones for fear of being robbed in broad daylight.

To get support, I decided to share this incident on my community page on Facebook. My friend and colleague Tosha Silver, author of *Outrageous Openness: Letting the Divine Take the Lead*, told me that this theft was a very positive omen. She told me that having that particular necklace snatched from me was a sign that the Goddess herself—in this case, in the form of Kali, the fierce goddess who takes you to the Underworld and transforms you—was now in charge of my trip. Kali often demands a sacrifice, she explained, and, in return, she helps you transform. Personally, I would have preferred an easier path—a more "fluffy" goddess. But that's not what my soul had in mind.

Enter Doris Cohen. I had had a number of readings with Dr. Cohen, who had pointed out to me, in her inimitable accent, that one of my colleagues was not doing me any favors. "She has you wrapped in barbed wire, my dear," Doris said. Now, Doris didn't know this person at all; in fact, she barely knew me. But she interpreted my problem accurately. And by putting a name to something I had felt but could not express, she helped me get myself out of a bad situation far sooner than I would have otherwise. So I knew that I could trust her judgment. And I knew that, in addition to her work with dreams, she also had decades of experience as a clinical psychologist. Many people are intuitives and psychics; but very few of them have rigorous training as psychologists. So very few of them know exactly how to interpret intuitive information in a practical and helpful way that their clients can actually hear and use.

When Doris heard the story of my necklace theft, she reached out to me and suggested that I send her my dreams from the following nights. She then gave me specific instructions about which nights to focus on. And, like the good student I am, I followed her instructions to the letter, sometimes getting up to record five or six dreams a night and sending them to her. I had been feeling as if I were alone in the desert, but accessing the wisdom in my dreams—with Doris's guidance—helped to ease my sorrow and heartbreak greatly.

Doris was a lifeline—a beam of light in one of the darkest three weeks of my life. I found that I was ill-suited to living my life at night—waking at 1:00 in the afternoon, then dancing until 6:00 in the morning; seeing only a bit of daylight each day, but walking for miles each night to and from dances and then waiting on the sidelines to be chosen as a partner. Doris's counsel brought comfort and sanity, and gave meaning to my suffering and my sorrow. Her ability to help me find the meanings of my dreams quite literally saved my sanity and my health. This book can do the same thing for you.

It was during that dark period—when I was concerned about my age, my desirability, my chance of ever finding love—that Doris reassured me that the goddess energy in women has nothing to do with age. In fact, in one of our sessions, she said: "My dear, goddesses never age." That statement—and the promise held within it—became a beacon for me, a beacon of hope and joy and possibility. That seed, planted deeply within me, eventually grew into my book *Goddesses Never Age: The Secret Prescription for Radiance, Vitality, and Well-Being*. This book and the PBS special derived from it have helped people all over the world rethink their approach to growing older and helped them see the truth in the words of Dr. Mario Martinez: "Growing older is inevitable. Aging is optional."

Kali took a gold goddess necklace from me. Abruptly. Violently. And then rewarded me many times over for being willing to go to the Underworld and return with pure treasure. My guide on this journey was Doris Cohen. Now, in this book, you can benefit from the same guidance. Doris helped me transform more than my own life. By extension, through my book, she helped me transform the lives of thousands of others all over the world. I owe her a huge debt of gratitude for teaching me that I can rely on my dreams to guide me through the inevitable times in life when I've found myself wandering in the desert, not knowing where to turn. Doris taught me that each dream is a mini-oasis that shows you where the water and food are located. You just need to know the language.

My dreamwork with Doris, which began in the middle of the night in Buenos Aires, continues to this day. And although I am no longer awash in sorrow and heartbreak—thanks, in large part, to that work—I still find that my dreams are loaded with energy and information that provide unique and magical guidance for my life

Every morning when I awaken, I spend a few moments in bed going over my dreams. Then I dictate them into my phone. I pay attention to the theme of each one and give each one a title—like a headline in a newspaper, just as Doris suggests. When appropriate, I even reenter a dream and change the outcome, just as Doris teaches. Later, when I have accumulated a number of dreams, I set up a time to go over them with Doris.

Through this process, I have become much more fluent in the language of my dreams. I have learned to access the magic of the night. And it is truly astounding. As Doris often reminds me, there is no time in the unconscious. And it's true. The more I do this kind of work, the more I realize that all time is *now,* and that, no matter when something happened, you can change your reaction to it, thereby changing your future.

Here's an example. I recently dreamed that I was at the funeral of one of my mother's oldest friends—we'll call her Carol. Carol, like my mother, believed that life without a husband was almost not worth living. Her own husband had died years before and she never recovered. Even though she was well-educated and had resources, she really believed there was no way you could enjoy going out to dinner, or staying at a fine hotel, or doing anything pleasurable if you weren't doing it with a man.

In the dream, one of the guests at the funeral started giggling when asked about her first sexual experience. She spoke of a sensation in her pelvis that was so unexpected she nearly fell over backward. I remember thinking that Carol's soul—looking on from beyond the veil—would find this very amusing. When I left Carol's house, I found that her dirt driveway and the road leading away from the house had been paved with beautiful costly stones. It looked lovely. All the stones, however, were placed on their edges, making it quite difficult to walk on them.

Dream title: "Carol's Funeral."

Dream story: Woman recounts first sexual experience with hilarity. New expensive rock road placed in front of house. Difficult to walk on.

Doris teaches that everyone in a dream is an aspect of the dreamer and that, in fact, the purpose of life—and of our dreams—is to heal the Self. So in this dream, Carol's funeral represents the death of the ideas she represented—that a woman living alone is somehow "less than." The beautiful stone road represents my soul's path as a pioneer in women's health. It is a very beautiful road, but it has cost me a lot and has been a difficult path to follow.

While discussing this dream with Doris, she suggested that I take a moment to celebrate the fact that my soul had actually done the work I had come to do, and that now that path could be much easier and more fun. What relief! In other words, because I'd done the work, I no longer had to continue walking on a difficult path.

Now it's your turn. You too can learn the secret language of the night and allow it to guide and heal your life. Remember that dreams are feedback from your soul. Where else can you access images, feelings, and guidance that are so uniquely your own? And your soul serves up this guidance to you night after night at absolutely no cost!

Everyone dreams. Now you have in your hands the "owner's manual" for how to work with your dreams fruitfully and in a way that is practical and simple. Read this book. Take it seriously. And begin your magnificent dream practice tonight. You'll be so glad you did.

CHRISTIANE NORTHRUP, MD, *February 4, 2017*

INTRODUCTION

Dreams have been described as messages from the Divine, manifestations of repressed emotion, and experiences from the collective unconscious. Edgar Cayce suggested that they come from spirit and healing, and involve spiritual growth. In a sense, all of these explanations have an element of truth to them. So why write this book? Because, with all that has been written on the interpretation of dreams, no one has yet brought this very important activity down to a level of practicality that can easily be applied to everyday waking life. It is as if someone were composing beautiful music or weaving the most beautiful stories for us every single night, and we were simply ignoring them. As a result, we seem to have lost our sense of the magic and amazement contained in our dreams.

One of the best definitions of dreams I've ever encountered comes not from a professional discussion at all, but from an article in *U.S. News and World Report*: "The experience of dreaming is as clearly universal as a heartbeat, and as individual as a fingerprint." I love it. It is simple, direct, and, like the world of the unconscious, offers rich possibilities for both the scientist and the poet. But what is it saying, really?

Not only do we all dream; we dream all the time. Research has shown that we dream five to eight dreams each night. Still, I very often hear people say: "Oh, I never dream." Or: "I used to dream, but I never dream now." No, no—it is simply that they do not remember their dreams.

Dreams are images and sensations, stories and inspirations. People are inspired in dreams to do the most amazing things in waking life.

The single most recorded song in history—the Beatles' "Yesterday," recorded hundreds of times by different artists, in different arrangements—resulted from a dream that inspired Paul McCartney to write the song. He simply woke up one morning, recalled the melody and lyrics he had heard in the dream, grabbed a pen, and wrote them down! The rest is history. Of course, Paul McCartney is not alone. When Elias Howe, inventor of the sewing machine, found himself struggling to come up with a way to thread a needle that would work with his machine's design, he had a dream that many others might have dismissed as a nightmare. He dreamed he was being held captive by a group of cannibals who were preparing to feast on him. As they danced about a fire, he noticed that their spears, which they were banging rhythmically up and down against the ground, featured small holes near the spearhead. When he woke, the vivid image of the holes and the rhythmic up-and-down motion of the spears led him to realize that installing the needle with the threading hole near the point that pierced the cloth would allow it to stitch continuously without tangling the thread. It was this discovery, inspired by a dream, that made his invention possible.

So where do these dreams come from? Throughout history, people have assumed many things about dreams. Some have belittled them as simply random collages of mental scraps, while others have subscribed to the grander notion that dreams are gifts from some external, spiritual force. These views began to change as people became better educated and developed their individual opinions and relationships. In fact, while dreams may at times have some aspects of both random collages or prophecy, the vast majority of your dreams are composed of information that exists in your individual unconscious.

The interpretation of the symbols that occur in our waking lives is, in fact, a link between our typical, conscious, left-brained way of interpreting information and the possibilities of interacting with the world from a right-brained perspective that is more actively engaged with the unconscious. The left brain represents your waking life, your conscious world. It comprises your analytical self and masculine energy, and controls the right side of your body. It represents the energy of the men in your life. Dreams, however, are mostly right-brain functions. The right side of your brain regulates your dreaming life—your unconscious world, your intuitive self—and the feminine energy that controls the left side of your body. Thus, when you dream, you're engaged with the energy of the women in your life. When you wake up, you cross from the unconscious world of the right brain into the conscious world of the left brain.

This crossing occurs both literally and figuratively. There is a band of nerves that connects the left brain and the right brain. Think of it as a bridge. When you wake, you cross that bridge from your dream life, where the language is symbolic—pictures, sensations, feelings, colors—to the conscious world of your analytical self, where the language is, well, actual language—verbal, literal, rational. Moving from the visual, symbolic world you inhabit each night into the verbal, literal world you inhabit during the day is as jarring as it might be to move in an instant from China to the United States. Imagine reading the rich poetry of China and suddenly finding yourself reading the *Wall Street Journal* as you taxi through Manhattan. Would you want to approach your Manhattan experience having discarded and forgotten all you'd learned while reading in China? This is, in a sense, what happens if you don't practice crossing the bridge between your right brain and your left brain. You wake up each morning having no tools with which to interpret and learn from the lessons that were presented to you in your dreams. And all those lessons and messages are irretrievably lost unless you learn to recall and explore them.

We all have the ability to recall more of our dreams, to understand them more deeply, and to apply all that we learn from them to our daily lives. Practice, or repetition of the process, can make you not just conversational in the language of symbols and the unconscious, but, with persistence, fluent in it. This fluency can help you make changes that will lead you to live a richer, fuller life—and it can do so quickly and easily. Moreover, by changing your own life, you begin to exert a measurable and positive influence on those around you and, ultimately, on all of humankind.

My own experience with the dramatic extent to which repetition and practice can help advance your understanding of dreams and the unconscious bears this out. I used to remember only about three dreams a year of the approximately 2000 to 3000 dreams each of us actually has each year. Many years ago, however, I joined a study group of like-minded people who gathered weekly to share and discuss their dreams, their goals, and spirituality in general. Each of us brought descriptions of our dreams for discussion. And this was how I learned both how to recall dreams and how to interpret them in ways that were helpful and directly applicable to my waking life. With practice and over a remarkably brief period of time (no more than three weeks), I learned to remember at least three dreams per week. With repetition and practice, I went from recalling three dreams a year to recalling over 150 dreams a year. While this is still just a fraction of the number of dreams we actually have each year, it was an encouraging start that led me to develop a process for dream recall and exploration that works like a charm.

This process is actually very simple. In fact, the only reason why most people don't regularly recall and analyze their dreams is that no one stresses to them the importance of dream recall. In our busy and technology-driven society, we are not trained to remember; we just don't have any practice remembering. In some cultures, it is traditional for people to sit around the breakfast table and speak of their dreams. People in these cultures have been practicing dream recall all their lives and can share and discuss their dreams with ease. In our culture, on the other hand, we wake up, jump out of bed, shower and get dressed, turn on the news, catch the latest blaring headlines, note the traffic and weather reports, listen to world events and terror alerts—and before we are even aware of it, we're totally absorbed in the waking world and our dreams are gone. Our engagement with the world of the unconscious is cut off, finished. We become completely immersed in the left side of our brains without having given ourselves a chance to pause, to cross the bridge between our unconscious and conscious worlds, and to consider what we've experienced and all we can learn from it.

Or maybe you do remember an occasional dream. Perhaps you've worried all day about a dream you had of your house catching fire and consulted a so-called "dream dictionary" to try and glean some meaning from the seemingly random images that came to you in that dream. Well, that, in my opinion, will get you nowhere. That is not what this book is about. While this book is about discovering what the images in your dreams mean to you personally, at its core, this is a book about learning the language of your unconscious, the language of symbols. Like the Divine, the unconscious speaks to us in symbols. By improving your fluency in the language of symbols, you not only become better able to interpret your dreams, you also establish a continuity between your conscious and unconscious worlds that enables you to use the language of symbols to understand your waking life better. Dreams are an entry point—the conduit through which you can begin to learn this language.

Unlike a spoken language, however, the language of symbols can not be contained in one convenient dictionary or grammar from which you can learn their meaning. There is no reference manual in the collective unconscious to help you accurately interpret your dreams and the symbols in them. Your personal and unique language of symbols cannot be defined by arbitrary definitions that someone else compiled. So-called "dream dictionaries" are thus worthless—although they still may have an element of truth in them that can mislead you into taking them seriously. In this book, I will not tell you what your dreams mean. You do not need anyone else to tell you what they mean. Rather, I want to help you discover their meaning for yourself—much as I have learned to do.

Over two decades ago, during a therapy session with a female patient, I had a sudden insight into what her dream might mean. I shared that insight with her and suddenly everything fell into place for her—the pieces fit together and made perfect sense. Everything we needed to understand her dream was right there, available to us. We applied the dream information to what was happening in her life and she left feeling much better. From that day on, every time I work on dreams, I remember the insight that encouraged me to connect the dots. And I have tried to bring that insight to bear on the more than 15,000 dreams I have worked to interpret since then—for my patients and clients, as well as for my family and friends. This important insight led me to develop the seven-step process presented here.

In Part I of this book, you will learn about the physiology and psychology of dreams, then explore the language of symbols in which they speak to us. In Part II, we'll examine the seven-step process for dream recall and exploration in detail and see how each step can lead you closer to understanding your dreams' symbolic messages. The steps are intentionally simple and easy to follow so that you can make them a part of your everyday routine without them becoming burdensome. Briefly, they are as follows:

Step 1. Recall and record your dream.

Step 2. Title your dream.

Step 3. Read or repeat your dream aloud, speaking slowly.

Step 4. Consider what is uppermost in your life right now.

Step 5. Describe the objects, characters, or qualities of your dream as if talking to a Martian.

Step 6. Summarize the message of your dream.

Step 7. Consider what guidance the dream offers.

In Part III, we'll examine how these steps have worked for others. In Part IV, you will begin to apply them to the interpretation of your own dreams.

Your dreams are valuable because they hold information from your unconscious that is directly related to you. Once you've recalled a dream, there are simple tools you can use to begin to make sense of it—tools that I will share with you in this book. My goal is to teach you how to approach your dreams using simple steps that can guide you through your own dreamwork. By following these simple steps, you can come to a clearer knowledge of your own unconscious life and, through that knowledge, gain a better understanding of your life in the world.

Part I

The ABCs
of Dreaming

CHAPTER 1

What Are Dreams?

Most people pay no attention to their dreams because of the prevailing notion that dreams are nothing more than noise in the brain—vestiges of waking experiences that linger in the nervous system. Let me be frank: That assumption is simply false. Yes, there are different patterns of waves in the brain, some of which relate to dreaming and some of which relate to our waking lives. But just because we do not yet know what dreams mean or their precise source does not mean that they are nothing but noise to be dismissed. This is one of the great failings of modern medicine—the assumption that not knowing the explanation for something means that there is no explanation for it.

The Tradition of Dreams

According to the Bible, dreams are prophetic and come from God. In ancient Egypt, priests traveled through different levels of consciousness to access what they referred to as the "magic library" in order to help petitioners interpret particularly vivid dreams. In ancient Greece, dreams were believed to come from Asclepius, the god of medicine. People suffering from imbalance or illness petitioned priests of Asclepius to interpret their dreams in order to heal them.

In modern times, Sigmund Freud opened the door to consideration of the unconscious by suggesting that dreams emerge from the unconscious as expressions of sexual urges and aggression suppressed in waking life. In fact, he referred to dreams as "the royal road to the unconscious." However, to interpret dreams as nothing more than disguises for our aggressive and sexual urges is intensely reductive and limits our humanity to a single dimension. After all, we are so much more than sex, than aggression. As expressions of divine energy, we are dreams, hopes, ideas, spirituality, play, and delight.

It was Carl Jung, extending the work of Freud, who spoke of the collective unconscious—a reservoir of experiences common to all humans—as the source of dreams. In other words, unlike Freud, he believed that dreams accessed something *beyond* the individual. Jung's insight did not, however, make it any easier for us to actually learn from our dreams. For, even if we are all connected through a collective unconscious, how can I make sense of messages I am accessing from the collective unconscious of someone in, say, rural China? I need to be concerned about *my* life, *my* experiences, so that I can change *me*. If you decide that dreams are only about the collective unconscious, it diminishes your personal relationship with your own unconscious. The truth is that our dreams are all about changing ourselves. Your dream is about *you* changing *you*. This is very important to keep in mind.

Today, many people believe that dreams are not prophecies, or repressions, or expressions of the collective unconscious, but are instead mere vestiges of things they have experienced during the day. Again, there is an element of truth to this. If you watch a movie about cowboys just before going to bed, you may fall asleep and dream that you are a cowboy, riding your horse into the sunset. When you wake up, you may dismiss your dream as meaningless, saying: "Well, I just watched a Western flick, and that explains why I had that dream." This may not be the case, however. You may have had a dream set in the context of the movie you watched before bed because embedding a message in that context makes it more likely that you will remember it the next day.

In other words, the unconscious uses events from your daily life as reinforcement. In this case, the message in the dream may be that you are on a journey and feel in charge. The message may have been delivered in a way that reenacts a part of your day, but the symbolic content would have been delivered one way or another, regardless of what you had experienced during the day. To enter the unconscious untethered is very scary. If, however, a movie connects to the unconscious and you dream of it, this provides a connection that makes the meaning easier for you to carry back with you into your conscious waking world.

The dreamer is always dreaming about the dreamer. So your dreams are always about you—*your* story, *your* life, and *your* conscious experiences. That is why they are often connected to what you are experiencing in your waking life—your relationships, hopes, expectations, and fears in the conscious world.

Types of Dreams

There are many types of dreams—big, small, thematic, recurring, even nightmares. The following is a list of the most common dreams you may experience.

* **Precognitive dreams**, in which you dream something that comes to pass in the future.

* **Intuitive dreams**, which are less specific than precognitive dreams and involve the sense that something may happen.

* **Warning dreams**, in which you are cautioned about something that is about to happen.

* **Health-related dreams**, in which you are presented with information about your own or someone else's health.

* **Pat-on-the-back dreams** that congratulate you on something you have achieved.

* **Pregnancy dreams** that may either be predictive of a physical pregnancy, or may indicate symbolically that you are preparing to give birth to new aspects of Self.

* **Death dreams**, in which you anticipate your own or someone else's death.

* **Past-life dreams,** in which you explore past lives through regression.

* **Nightmares,** in which you experience your deepest fears.

* **Recurring dreams,** which bring you important messages about potentially troubling patterns in your life.

* **Guidance dreams,** which can help you make decisions or changes in your life.

* **Lucid dreams,** in which you are conscious that you are in a dream state.

Many people tend to see precognitive dreams as predictive. This is not necessarily so, and is certainly not so in a constraining or limiting sense. Precognitive dreams may tell you about something that, in fact, happens in the future. But they never constrain your conscious life. They never present events or situations that *must* occur in the future. I generally try not to emphasize precognitive dreams because, frankly, dreams that are truly precognitive are rare. Unfortunately, however, many people begin to think all of their frightening dreams are precognitive and become terrified. So it is not a good idea to assume that your dreams foretell the future, because it is at the level of symbolism, not literal interpretation, that your dreams communicate most clearly and urgently.

Here is an example of a precognitive dream that I experienced myself that illustrates this. In 1980, I was in a car accident and hurt my back. As I was recovering, I dreamed that my father, who was healthy and fully functioning at the time, was in a wheelchair. I became very upset and overwhelmed, sure that the dream predicted he would become paralyzed. Then, in 1982, he had a physical episode similar to a stroke and was unconscious for ten days. When he regained consciousness and began to heal, I asked him why he came back. He responded that he came back so that he could continue to help and support his family and his people. He went on living for another nine years. The last year of his life was very difficult for him. He was confined to a wheelchair—not paralyzed, but very ill.

This was in 1990, so my dream was clearly precognitive in a sense. Yet even in this dream of my father, there was useful symbolic information that went beyond the merely predictive. The wheelchair represented limitation. To me, my father represented complete and unwavering faith. When I had the dream, I was recovering from an accident and was in a lot of pain. So in my dream, my faith was so injured that it had to be confined to a wheelchair. In other words, I was in great pain and discomfort and filled with the fear that I would never recover—that I would have to live out my life in pain. Ultimately, however, that pain led me to holistic healing and care, to discovering the relationship of the body to the self, which was an important revelation for me and helped me to become healthier. Without it, I would not have had the motivation to explore holistic healing.

No matter what type of dream you experience, the important thing to remember is that the dreamer is always dreaming about the dreamer. So your dreams are always about *you*. They function as a bridge from the conscious world of your own everyday waking life to the world of your own unconscious—and back again. Their messages, therefore, always deliver information about *you*—information that you can apply in practical ways when you know how to decipher its meaning. In the next chapter, we'll look at how the brain perceives and delivers these messages, and how you can begin to use the information to move forward in your waking life.

* * * * * * * * * * * * * * * * *

To sum up...

1. Dreams function as a bridge between the conscious and unconscious worlds.

2. The dreamer is always dreaming about the dreamer. So your dreams are always about *you*.

3. There are many different types of dreams, each with a different symbolic function.

4. Precognitive dreams are never predictive in a limiting sense, although they may present possibilities for future action.

CHAPTER 2

The Physiology
of Dreams

Everything in the world can be perceived as a wave, a cycle—
everything from the waves of the ocean to the phases of the
moon. Sleep and dreams are no different. We fall asleep; we
dream; we awaken. All the while, our brains are also experiencing cycles in which our brain waves operate more quickly or more
slowly. The phase in which we are active, awake, and speaking is called
the *beta* phase. In the beta phase, your brain operates at approximately
twelve to forty-eight cycles per second. The next phase is called the
alpha phase, in which your brain waves operate at a wider and slower
amplitude, approximately eight to twelve cycles per second. In this
phase, you can perform self-hypnotic suggestion, a variation of which
can help with the recollection of dreams—a process we will discuss and
practice later.

The transition between the beta and alpha phases is what leads
to the sudden sensation of falling that sometimes propels you from a
light sleep. The reason you have this sensation and then startle yourself
awake is simply that, as you enter the alpha phase—as you go deeper
into the unconscious—you experience a disconnect between your brain

waves and your body. Sometimes, your body does not keep pace with your mind's relaxation, which leads to the feeling of falling and sudden awakening. Once you give yourself the opportunity to fall asleep again, you likely do so more readily.

Following the alpha phase of brain activity comes the *theta* phase, in which you are fully asleep and your brain waves operate at about two to eight cycles per second. And finally, beyond this phase is the *delta* phase, in which you are deeply asleep, your brain waves operating at only about one-half to one cycle per second. As you sleep through the night, your brain passes into and out of these phases: from alpha through theta, then delta, then back up through theta and alpha, and so on. Each dream is a cycle, and you pass through approximately five to eight of these cycles each night as you sleep. Thus, you dream five to eight dreams per night. This is fairly typical for most adults, unless they are taking medication, which may dampen dreams to some extent. We will discuss some of the effects of medications later—both prescription medicines like antidepressants and antianxiety drugs, and substances used for self-medication, like alcohol or marijuana. These can all have an impact, not just on your body, but on your dreams.

Remarkably, those who habitually meditate—monks, for example—can go into the delta phase of brain activity and still remain completely awake. Studies have shown that, although they are completely awake and alert, their brain waves are cycling at a very slow rate. This indicates that they have full and amazing control over both their bodies and their unconscious minds, since they can inhabit the unconscious and still function in the waking world. Meditation is a wonderful tool that works very well to calm the mind and bring peace. In our modern world, however, spending hours on end in daily meditation is not a very practical solution to most of our everyday problems. That is why we need swifter, simpler, deeper, sharper tools for reaching the unconscious.

The reason that we pass through these sleep cycles each night is, in part, to ensure physical restoration. When you experience REM (rapid eye movement) sleep, it enhances learning and memory at the physiological, cellular level. Sleep scientists used to believe that dreams only occurred during REM sleep, but have discovered through research that they do, in fact, occur even in non-REM states. They found in their studies that people awakening from deep-sleep states like theta or delta were having dreams, even though their eyes were not moving back and forth under their eyelids (which is what characterizes REM sleep). They were able to confirm this by monitoring people's brain waves as they slept. Non-REM dreaming occurs primarily in the deepest phase of sleep—that is, the delta phase. To emerge from delta sleep, your brain must travel all the way up through the theta phase and into the alpha phase, which is why we tend to remember more of our REM dreams. Dreams experienced in delta sleep are distant and difficult to recall, because this sleep is so very deep.

Sleep and Your Health

An entire science and industry centered on rejuvenation and antiaging is emerging all across the world that centers on the potency of growth hormones. This is important for us to note here, because delta-phase and non-REM dreaming are involved in the synthesis of proteins and the release of these growth hormones. Applied to everyday life, this means that, if you do not allow yourself to sleep long enough and deeply enough, your body will not release as much growth hormone. This is detrimental because growth hormone facilitates both physical and emotional growth, up to and including the cellular level. You release this hormone in abundance during infancy; but when you reach your early twenties, its release begins to diminish. Throughout your life, however, the release of this hormone is promoted by deep sleep. In a normal sleep cycle, you start out in beta and then descend through alpha and theta before reaching the delta phase. But it requires time to reach the deeper phases. If you are not sleeping for long enough periods, you may not reenact the sleep cycles as reliably. Instead of experiencing five to eight cycles per night, you may at best pass through one or two, or you may never reach the delta phase at all. The result is that you will not release sufficient revitalizing growth hormone to maintain your health.

Lack of deep sleep has other detrimental effects on your body as well—for instance, in the area of weight control. When you do not sleep deeply enough, you do not calm your bodily systems enough. Consequently, your adrenals don't get enough rest and continue to release cortisol, which affects your insulin levels. This can lead to chronic insulin spikes, or even problems with insulin release. If insulin is not released properly, your insulin and sugar levels become imbalanced and you start putting on weight, because, when your insulin levels are not balanced, nearly everything you consume is deposited as fat. Excess cortisol sends your brain this message: "I am in stress and need more energy. Therefore, please deposit the food I digest as fat so that I will have extra energy to face this crisis." It's just the way we are wired.

It generally requires six to eight hours of deeper sleep for most of us to maintain our health. If you have convinced yourself that you cannot "waste" six to eight hours each night, just remember that giving yourself sufficient time to reach deeper sleep stages is utterly essential for your physical health, your hormonal health, your looks, your youthfulness, your weight, your brain, your mind, your heart, your pancreas, your liver—yes, I could go on. Do you consider replenishing your body and mind to be a waste of time? Probably not. So try to get six to eight hours of sleep each night.

I acknowledge that, for many people, simply remaining asleep for six to eight hours can be challenging. So how can you find a healthy balance? Begin by making a decision to proceed gradually. Set yourself a goal and then phase into it. For the first week or so, aim each night to get at least five hours of sleep. After you have done this for a week or two, move on and increase your goal to six hours.

Taking a "siesta" can also be a useful technique. In Spain, for instance, everything shuts down in the afternoon. Everyone goes home, eats the day's main meal, and then sleeps for two to three hours. Later, in the evening, they resume their activities, dining as late as 10 or 11 o'clock at night. The wisdom of this lifestyle goes beyond adaptation to a warm climate. Research has shown that, around 2 o'clock in the afternoon, your body enters a cycle in which you become very sleepy. Your thyroid starts slowing down, and then everything in your body slows down, giving your system a chance to rest before your energy level begins to rise again. You may feel hungry and want to take a break, or to slow down, calm down, and rest. In our fast-moving Western society, however, many of us must work straight through to 5 o'clock, so we have another cup of coffee or a cigarette, or we eat something sugary or drink an energy drink. This goes against the body's natural cycle, however. In this cycle, you have more energy in the morning, when hormones are being released to prepare you for activity. Your energy starts to wane mid-afternoon and then begins to rise again approximately two hours later. So if you really want to follow the cycles and natural rhythms of your mind and body, you should rest in the mid-afternoon.

Learning to take power naps can help to mitigate a lack of deep sleep. You can train yourself to benefit from these naps by doing deep-breathing exercises. Close your eyes and imagine that you are sitting beneath a large and shady tree on the edge of a lake or stream. Just breathe in and out. Your brain is a creature of habit and learns by repetition. Its first reaction to this exercise may thus be something like: "Wait a minute, this is a different pattern. I have to get back to normal, so I better wake up." Even if you wake up, however, do not get up. Pause, and take another few deep breaths. Go back into the shade, breathing in and out.

Because you are used to working, to constantly doing, your brain has learned to keep you prepared for a habitually frenetic pace. The trick is to move past the automatic responses of your body and retrain the amygdala—the midbrain, which modulates cortisol release—to calm down, to rest. Your adrenals may be racing, giving messages to your thyroid to kick in; your mind may resist, urging you to go, go, go. But, even if you are jerked back to full consciousness, just keep breathing slowly in and out for five to ten minutes. Even if you stay conscious throughout that time, do not worry. If you adopt the technique gradually, your brain will have a less difficult time adjusting. If you push too hard, try to change too drastically or too quickly, your brain will just refuse to cooperate. The brain learns by repetition and is responding to one of God's most important laws—the Law of Conservation of Energy. The brain wants to conserve energy, so it does what it knows how to do. It resists new methods because it has to apply substantially more energy to learn new patterns.

Despite some people's insistence that they do not dream, it is not possible not to experience some REM sleep. In fact, if you are sleep-deprived, you will experience even more REM dreams, because your unconscious will try to make up for the deprivation. In the 1950s, a radio-show host in New York decided to forgo sleep for as long as he could, reporting on his experience all the while. He remained awake for about seven days, always under the care of a physician. However, like most people at that time, doctors did not really understand enough about dreaming or sleep deprivation to protect the radio host's health. As a consequence, he became so disoriented, so disturbed, that it nearly ended his marriage and he almost committed suicide. As the time passed, he became increasingly hyperemotional and totally out of control.

When you do not allow your brain to go into a REM state, to go down through the sleep cycles, it reacts by forcing you to make up for it during the day. So the radio host began to enter the unconscious world during the day. Because he was technically awake, however, he did not even realize that he was experiencing a waking dream. This led him to feel and sound disoriented—crazy. The nonsequential unconscious was emerging even as he was trying to approach his work and relationships consciously and rationally. That is, although there was nothing crazy about what was happening, it felt crazy, because the parameters of the unconscious are so different.

If you are like most people, you may have experienced a mild version of this. If you have not slept properly, you may startle suddenly, as if you had been sleeping, although you are awake. Most people experience these "pop-ups" in the late afternoon, when their brain waves slow down enough that they begin to reenact the REM sleep they have missed for several nights in a row in an attempt to initiate physical and psychological restoration.

A patient described this occurring over weekly dinner at her mother's house. "When we're done eating, she talks while she gets up and does things in the kitchen. And suddenly, I'm not there. My eyes are open and I'm listening to her, but suddenly I'll see something totally unconnected to what she is saying—a school bus, driving kids, going down a hill. Then I actually have a physical response. My whole body jerks, and she says that I am falling asleep at the table. Of course, I deny it, but she is right." This kind of experience is similar to being asleep and having a dream. Perhaps my friend allows herself to enter that state more comfortably when she is safe with her mother, or because she is full from dinner and feels she can finally relax.

Dreams—and healthy sleep patterns—are thus an important part of leading a healthy and productive life. Above and beyond the messages that they deliver from your unconscious, they play an important role in keeping your body healthy and your life in balance. In the next chapter, we will examine how dreams also play an important part in keeping your mind healthy and balanced.

* * * * * * * * * * * * * * * *

To sum up...

1. Sleep cycles regulate important bodily functions that affect your health.

2. Dreams are an important part of the cycles that regulate sleep.

3. Most dreams occur in REM (rapid eye movement) sleep, but they can also occur in non-REM states.

4. Sleep deprivation, and the resulting lack of dreams, can have adverse effects on both your waking life and your health.

CHAPTER 3

The Psychology
of Dreams

D reams speak to you in the language of the unconscious. But hallucinations are another way in which the unconscious speaks to you. If your everyday structure, your everyday life, is not very stable, you may move between the conscious and unconscious worlds uncontrollably. Doctors call it schizophrenia or psychosis. Psychosis, however, is simply not realizing that you are relating to the conscious world via the unconscious. I do not say this dismissively. Studies have shown that, when people are deprived of sleep or stimulation (sensory deprivation, or immersion in a tank of warm water with no light or sound), they enter a state of altered consciousness; they begin to hallucinate.

We tend to characterize all hallucinations as inherently bad. We medicate people who hallucinate and deem them psychotic. And, of course, hallucinations can be overwhelming and dangerous. However, not all hallucinations are pernicious. Hallucination is, in fact, nothing but a waking dream state. In many cases, it may not be detrimental, but rather a manifestation of the mind and body seeking balance. Balance is the universal law. The body is always seeking homeostasis, much as a thermostat does. Before they turned digital, older thermostats had a mercury bar that acted in two different ways. When the temperature warmed up, the mercury thickened and rose, triggering a response in the mechanism it was controlling. When the temperature cooled, the process was reversed. The body works in much the same way. When you are deprived of sleep (and, by extension, dreams) or stimulation, your body generates dreamlike images and stimulation for you in an attempt to restore balance.

Researchers have determined the frequency of dreaming among various age groups using tools like electrodes to monitor REM sleep. Their studies show that infants demonstrate the most brain activity, while the elderly who are senile or suffering from dementia dream the least. The frequency of our dreams apparently diminishes as we reach the end of our lives, probably because our conscious brain activity may be so low that we have already partially crossed over into the world of the unconscious. Infants and children, on the other hand, who are just beginning life and whose brains are just beginning to develop, dream more frequently. When we dream, our bodies synthesize proteins, building and developing cells throughout the nervous system and the entire body. This synthesis is an essential and profound function that takes place when we sleep—and when we dream.

It is interesting that people who have attempted suicide typically tend to dream more. It is as if, after attempting to enter the world of the unconscious—the world of death, the world of the unknown—their dreams become more meaningful because they rely on the unconscious to help them deal with fears and feelings in the conscious world. It is as if the unconscious were saying: "Take it easy, take it easy. Do not do this; you're going to be okay. Let me tell you some stories that will show you some of the issues you must face to move on." In a sense, it is as if their souls speak to them through the unconscious. Those who, in previous lives, have attempted to take or have taken their own lives invariably flirt with suicide in this life. They think about it, or believe they want to pursue it. But if they consider it too seriously or go so far as to attempt it, the unconscious—the soul—delivers a stern message: "Don't do this; there are so many feelings assailing you. But if you pay attention, you can heal." Similarly, people who experience depression also dream more—perhaps because they are so disengaged from daily life. They are not doing enough conscious work during the day, so that work takes place at night through the unconscious.

Our dreams access the spiritual realm in which God's laws pertain. And one of the essential laws of divine energy is the Law of the Pendulum—every soul seeking balance. We tend to swing from one extreme to another, like a pendulum, because our souls are always trying to balance somewhere in the center. If you are depressed during the day—oppressed by your conscious life and feeling down—your unconscious will try to make up for it as you sleep. Put simply, what you do not consciously express in the waking world, your unconscious makes up for by expressing it in the dream world.

This is why people who take antidepressants typically have very intense and violent dreams. Antidepressants may lift the mood a little, but they often dampen other energies in the process—energies like sexuality, passion, joy, and a love of life. People taking antidepressants often find life bearable, but uninspiring, devoid of strong feelings. Think about all the things that inspire strong feelings in you—people, creatures, objects, events—everything from avoidance to amazement or adoration. Then imagine feeling indifferent to them. God didn't create us and this amazing world so that we would go through life feeling indifferent to it. When your passion, your ardor for life, is dampened during the day, it makes sense that your unconscious mind delivers more intense and vivid dreams to make up for the lack of intensity while you are conscious and awake.

Psychological Disorders

Throughout my career, I have heard thousands of what I call "non-explanations" for psychological disorders. A patient who is bipolar suffers from a brain imbalance. But this is not an explanation. The real question is: Why is the brain imbalanced? And what about diseases like multiple sclerosis or Parkinson's? Yes, they all indicate an imbalance in the brain. But, again, what caused the imbalance? When we create imbalances in the brain—perhaps through mistakes in judgment when younger, dampening pain in the psyche with overindulgence or self-medication with drugs or alcohol—the brain expresses it. As we get older, our bodies begin to express those traumas in the form of various ailments. Similarly, when your waking life is dampened, your unconscious steps in and begins to exaggerate the feelings you are tamping down in order to get your attention and make up for that avoidance.

A particular type of antidepressant, SSRIs, frequently leads to insomnia as well as increased sweating. Just as the unconscious releases the emotions suppressed during the daytime, the body on SSRIs releases all that pent-up energy through your skin as sweat, which is simply the release (or "expression") of toxicity. People on SSRIs also have an increased frequency of periodic involuntary limb movements, as if the body—deprived of emotion and movement—is prompted by the unconscious to compensate. In fact, they often end up on other medications to help mitigate the side effects of the antidepressant—for example, medication to relieve Restless Leg Syndrome. This is problematic, however, because it addresses the side effects and symptoms without addressing the source of the problem. SSRIs can cause a drastic reduction in REM sleep and an increase in nightmares. Over time, people taking them may fall into a REM state while awake, during the daytime. Sleep paralysis is normal during dreaming; however, SSRIs interfere with this process and those who take them may appear awake and move while they are actually in a deep-sleep state.

Conversely, people start to dream less frequently after undergoing my therapy, because we focus on retrieving information from the unconscious and applying it to waking life. I have observed this repeatedly and directly in my work with my patients. When you pay close attention to both your conscious life and your unconscious, your unconscious doesn't need to knock on the door seven times to get your attention. The artist Salvador Dali once commented that he used to have dreams, but stopped at some point—perhaps because he had shared the messages of his unconscious through his expressive art. Similarly, when my patients share dreams by working through them with me and then make appropriate changes in their conscious lives, their unconscious minds don't have to knock as many times or as loudly.

Another way in which dreams provide psychological restoration and balance appears in the fact that pregnant women who have more nightmares during pregnancy have lower incidences of postpartum depression. Expectant mothers sometimes dream that they give birth to a mentally disabled or disfigured child, or one afflicted with some sort of terrible illness. These dreams are simply an indication that those fears exist and need to be expressed and faced. Once the child is born, the mother is less apt to succomb to depression, because she has expelled her fears in sleep.

Dreams and the Conscious Mind

The frontal lobes of the brain—the neo-cortex—are where we think consciously, where we make adult decisions. Although these areas do not develop fully until we are between twenty-three and twenty-five years old, they start developing more fully at the age of thirteen—an age at which many cultures celebrate a coming of age. This is just one instance of how spirituality, intuition, and science often synchronize with and affirm one another. When you dream, the prefrontal cortex shuts down. That is, your consciousness, your decisions, your choices shut down. What comes alive during dreaming is the midbrain—the limbic system—which controls emotion and memory.

The midbrain is where you experience the fight-or-flight response, aggression, and desire. It is interesting that our sense of smell, the oldest sense in terms of evolution, is the only sense with a direct connection to the hypothalamus, the emotional center. This is why scents can provoke such powerful memories and responses. Remember, the upper regions of the brain shut down when you dream, because they are where you make rational, conscious decisions—logical decisions and choices in conscious time. This is what allows you to enter the amazing world of the unconscious, a world in which the limbic system and unfiltered emotions are activated.

When you dream, it enhances your learning and memory. And, of course, infants and children have much to learn—everything from language to a sense of self. Extensive research has been done to determine the best way to learn things and these studies have affirmed the value of dreaming to the learning process. In some studies, subjects learned very irrelevant, trivial bits of information (random numbers and details, simple instructions for performing a task, etc.), then fell asleep. When they awoke, they were asked to recall the information. Those who dreamed invariably remembered the information better than those who did not dream—even when the dreams in question had absolutely nothing to do with the information they had learned.

Dreams have other interesting effects on your brain centers as well. For instance, if you dream about pillaging, or plundering, or something terrifying and destructive, your body wants to act on this. But if you were to act, it could be very dangerous. So your brain actually shuts down certain areas to keep you from physically expressing what you are experiencing in your dream. Discharging this energy in a dream is much safer and easier than doing so while you are awake.

This is what happens in sleep paralysis, which occurs when you emerge from a dream but are not yet fully awake. That is, your brain is trying to wake up, but your body is still obeying instructions, telling it to remain paralyzed so that you can continue dreaming. A disconnect, a disharmony, occurs because you are beginning to become aware. Your brain is moving into the theta and alpha phases, moving from an unconscious to a conscious state. Your mind, your consciousness and awareness, may be in an alpha state, but your body is still being governed by the unconscious, unable to act on physical impulses. You may feel as if you are paralyzed, but it's simply a matter of your mind moving too swiftly from one state to another and your body not having caught up yet.

Sleep paralysis should happen infrequently, although there are emotional issues that may trigger it to occur more often—a feeling of paralysis in waking life, a feeling of being constrained or locked up. Metaphorically, you are aware that you are awake, but you feel completely paralyzed in your life. So you experience both a conscious and an unconscious state—and your body responds to both.

The neocortex, the frontal lobe, is also the center of your episodic memory. It is the center of your waking, adult life, where you remember things and experience cognition, judgment, and choices. When you dream, you set aside conscious choices, decisions, and rational judgments, because you are moving into the unconscious, where everything is based on and communicated through symbols. This allows you to travel into the reality of your dreams, the unconscious reality, where anything is possible and messages can be conveyed in images that defy logic. I can meet the president; you can leap like a gazelle. These things could not take place in the upper regions of the brain where you think rationally as an adult, where everything is based in common sense and logical expression. But when those areas shut down, the unconscious can communicate using the language of symbols without being limited by what is or is not possible, what does or does not make sense, in waking life.

The unconscious world where dreams occur is a place without time or limits, where the *lingua franca* is the language of symbols. In the next chapter, we'll explore this rich and profound language and learn how it can become a powerful influence on your everyday waking life.

* * * * * * * * * * * * * * * *

To sum up...

1. Hallucinations are expressions of a waking dream state.

2. Dreams regulate our conscious and unconscious worlds according to the law of balance.

3. Mental disorders indicate an imbalance in the relationship between our conscious and unconscious worlds.

4. The world of the unconscious is a place without time or limits where everything is possible.

CHAPTER 4

The Language of Symbols

Interpreting dreams is really very simple. We tend to make it seem more complex simply because we do not know how to go about it. When I told one publisher about my commitment to write this book, he said: "It will never sell." It was as if someone had slapped me in the face. But I was determined to find a way around the obstacle. The simplest thing would have been to consider calling the book something that didn't directly relate to dream analysis. The reason such books do not sell is that none of them actually help people to understand their dreams, and certainly not in a simple, direct way that they can use every day. The books may be interesting, but they do not teach.

On the other hand, I wanted my book to be like a workshop, a teaching manual that could enable and encourage the practice of dreamwork centered on dreamers themselves—on what your dreams mean to you, not my ideas or anyone else's ideas about what a given symbol does or should mean to you. And even dream books that are somewhat helpful describe methods that are just too complicated. Who is going to sit down and meditate for twenty minutes every day and then write for another twenty minutes about each dream they have? It's too much to ask of people and too hard to stick with. My many years working as a therapist have shown me that, when we make processes too complex, people simply give up or just don't continue to practice them.

True, the left brain is where 1 + 1 is always 2, whether you see it in space or in a mathematics book, whether you are playing with marbles or eating cookies. But the language of the unconscious determines 95 percent of our behavior and that's controlled by the right brain, which is not logical at all. Logic is not the main dynamic in the language of symbols, dreams, art, or the unconscious. The world of symbols is where 1 + 1, and what it represents, depends entirely on context, feeling, color, and setting. Symbols are only hard to understand because we never learn their language. I have been fortunate. I was exposed to many different languages throughout my life, so I have had to exercise both sides of my brain. Hebrew and Arabic are read and written from right to left; English and Spanish from left to right. But they all make sense to their own speakers.

This is why people who grow up speaking Chinese and Japanese have an advantage over Westerners when it comes to understanding the language of symbols. Their languages are conveyed in characters and pictures. Pictures access the right brain; words access the left. Languages like Chinese and Japanese combine the two. The Divine gave us brains with two sides so we could use both. So, in a sense, when we ignore our dreams, we are ignoring God's messages to us. Not in a prophetic sense, of course, but in a symbolic sense. I often hear people saying that God spoke to them. Although these experiences may seem very real to them and they may feel a real sense of connection to the Divine, this is really about the language of symbols expressing whatever is important to that individual personally. God communicates with us through the language of symbols all the time. But so do our dreams. And understanding what is going on in your dreams can help you understand this language—and make your waking life so much richer.

Life can be defined as movement. And, as we said before, everything in life occurs in waves or cycles. Music is measured in waves, as are light, sound, and vibration. When you are depressed or feeling down, you can always think of the analogy of the wave and reassure yourself that you will soon start to come back up again. And when you understand the language of the unconscious, you can accomplish this in your dreams as well as in your conscious life.

It's All About You

The language of symbols is specific to both personal experience and to historical and cultural context. There are a number of dream books that discuss, for instance, how Native Americans interpret dreams. This may be very interesting and a rich source of historical context, but how does it help me in my life? I live in the current day and I am not, myself, Native American. So how is this relevant to me? In some tribes, it was a morning tradition to share dreams among their families or groups. In these tribes, the shaman—the one who had the best connection with the unconscious—was described as "going underground" to interpret dreams. By symbolically going underground, he was accessing darker places of awareness, places in the unconscious. Now, if I were part of that tribe or lived in a Native American culture, this method of dream interpretation would be directly applicable to my dreams and therefore to my life. But I'm not; and I don't; and therefore it is not.

When you begin to work on your dreams, you make sense of them by making connections between your *own* unconscious and your *own* conscious world. Think of your conscious life as today's newspaper— *The Daily Dreamer.* When you begin to make connections to it by interpreting your dreams, you give your dream a title—a headline— and then determine what is going on right this very instant in your life that relates to that headline. After you've read the article, so to speak, and learned what it is about, it is time to editorialize. What are you going to do about what you have learned? When you begin to pay attention to dreams and use what you learn in them to make changes in your waking life, your dreams become less insistent and you may actually begin to recall fewer dreams. People who have done rigorous dreamwork often become perturbed because they suddenly cannot remember their dreams. But this is a positive sign! It means that they are working actively on their unconscious by working on their conscious lives.

According to one tradition—the Jewish Kabbalah— if you want to ask a question of someone who has died, you go to the cemetery, ask your question, and later receive the answer in a dream. When you think about it, this makes sense, because, in a cemetery, everyone is dead; they've already crossed over into the realm of the unconscious. To elicit a dream there draws on an energy divorced from conscious life. The symbolism behind the tradition is thus grounded in the difference between the conscious world and the unconscious. When you are in a cemetery, you are surrounded by the unconscious. And that helps to elicit messages from your own unconscious.

When you go to the tomb of someone you love, you connect with them. Perhaps you go there to ask a question. Or perhaps you go there just to pay your respects and to mourn. You may cry. Why is this important? Because crying is an expression of emotions. Crying helps you release your emotions. And emotion is itself a life force. In fact, the only thing that doesn't have emotion is a corpse. You may feel emotionless; you may not be expressing your emotions at certain times. Nonetheless, as long as there is life, there is emotion. E-motion is energy in motion.

Learning the Language of Dreams

The language of dreams is the language of symbols, and the world needs to start learning that language. Dreams may be messages about your everyday life; but they can also be warnings or guidance. The Bible tells of the Pharaoh who dreamed of seven skinny cows eating up seven fat cows; then he dreamed of seven overflowing bags of wheat being gobbled up by seven nearly empty bags. Nobody could interpret his dreams until Joseph, a prisoner unjustly detained, came along, listened to the dreams, and told the Pharaoh that there would be seven years of plenty followed by seven years of famine. This warning prompted the Pharaoh to store as much food as possible during the years of plenty to prepare for the years of famine. Moreover, this dream of warning also provided a solution for the problem—the overflowing bags of wheat being consumed by the empty ones. All it took was someone conversant in the language of symbols to figure it out. That's the richness of dreams.

How do we determine what is simply symbolic, what is a warning, what is guidance, and what is prophecy? We learn it over time, just as when we learn a new language. You learn a new language in your conscious life through practice. You learn simple words first, then more complicated words, and then phrases. And then you put the phrases together into sentences. You become more and more familiar with the meaning of the words and the phrases by practicing them and applying them to the world you see around you. The same is true as you begin to learn the language of the unconscious—the language of symbols.

If you've never worked with dreams before, it can all seem very strange. But there are some simple steps that can guide you to greater clarity. The first order of business is to record your dreams. Practice recording them every morning when you awaken, whether you use a tape recorder or notebook. In fact, start by saying aloud three times as you fall asleep: "I'll remember my dreams clearly and well." This can trigger your unconscious to prompt you to record your dreams faithfully.

When a friend of mine turned sixteen and got her license, her father decided to teach her how to drive safely in the snow. After a hefty snowfall, he took her to an empty parking lot and told her: "You have to make the car go out of control so that you can learn to control it." By facing the terrifying feeling of losing control in a safe, supportive environment, my friend learned how to respond to that feeling in a way that was effective. This is a wonderful metaphor for working with your dreams. By facing situations and feelings in the unconscious, where you are safe from physical harm, you learn to respond to your fears and worries more calmly and effectively in your conscious life. So don't be afraid. Go out of control in a safe environment; learn how to manage it. Then go forward with confidence, because you will have acquired the tools that can help you move beyond the fear.

It is very difficult to learn anything effectively when you are nervous or excited. When you are stressed, you act from your midbrain responses—you are in fight-or-flight mode. That is not the time to learn; it's the time to survive. The time to learn is when you are calm and safe, when your mind is clear and open. Learning occurs when information comes into your awareness. But how can you take information in when you're thinking only about survival, or focused only on how you can escape a situation?

Dreams as Stories

We are all instinctive storytellers—perhaps a vestige of a time when we sat around fires in caves or huts and told stories as a way of sharing our experiences. And the process of storytelling remains very important as a means of conveying information. If you want to teach a principle, tell a story. Our brains have been conditioned by evolution to take in information in this way. Stories, rich as they are in symbols and metaphors, are an effective way to access the unconscious, because they, in fact, emerge from the unconscious. This is why children respond so fully when you tell them stories, even if they don't know exactly what the story means. The story of the *Wizard of Oz* has entralled children for generations not because they understand its deeper symbolic meaning, but because they relate it to their own life experiences.

When you begin to explore your dreams, you don't have to tell a wonderful story. Your dream story may be as simple as: "There is a bottle on the sink and it is filled with soap." The point is that, when you tell the story, the information it contains travels into your unconscious, where you can learn from it.

The language of symbols forms a bridge that can carry you from the world of your everyday waking life into the timeless and limitless world of the unconscious—and back again. In Part II, you will learn how you can use my simple seven-step system to begin interpreting the symbolic messages sent to you by your unconscious through your dreams.

* * * * * * * * * * * * * * * * *

To sum up...

1. Dreams speak to us in the language of symbols.

2. The dreamer is always dreaming about the dreamer. So your dreams are always about you and the symbols in them always relate to your own experiences.

3. We learn the language of symbols just as we learn any other language—through practice.

4. Dreams are stories that give us important information through the language of symbols.

Part II

The Seven Steps of Dream Recall and Exploration

CHAPTER 5

Step 1. Recall and Record Your Dream

As a result of my many years of practice working with people to help them interpret and learn from their dreams, I have developed this seven-step process that can guide you as you begin to recall and explore your own dream world. The process for doing this is really quite simple, although it will take some practice before you are adept at it.

First, you must set yourself a goal and stay focused on it. I recommend starting with the goal of recording and interpreting one dream per week. As you begin, there are two important things to remember:

* *Never overthink your dream story;* don't judge what you remember from your dream. Just observe your dream and embrace its message. This is what I call the "observe and embrace rule."

* *The dreamer is always dreaming about the dreamer.* Regardless of what characters, objects, events, or settings may appear in them, your dreams are always about you.

There are several small steps you can take to make the process of remembering and recording your dreams simpler. After all, if you are going to stick with it, you need a process that fits into your life without becoming burdensome. The first step, of course, is to put a notebook and pen or a voice recorder by your bed. It does not matter which you use—just choose whatever method makes you most comfortable.

As soon as you awaken from sleep—before you even get up to go to the bathroom—note the date on your pad or your recorder and relate whatever you can remember about your dreams. Do this as swiftly as possible. If all you recall is "a patch of blue," that's fine; don't overthink it. Just write it down or record it, keeping in mind that this should be done quickly. If you absolutely cannot remember anything, try closing your eyes for just a few moments to see if pieces of a dream come back to you. Remember, when you first awaken, you are still in alpha phase and thus closer to the unconscious and the memories of your dreams. Once you have recorded all that you can remember, simply set the dream story aside and start your day.

Now let's talk about how you can begin to remember more of your dreams, so that you have something a little more substantial to work with in the morning. To facilitate your dream recall, try practicing the following steps before you fall asleep—when you are at the other end of the dream experience. After you lie down and feel you are beginning to fall asleep—not when you first get into bed, when your brain is likely still in beta phase—you enter what is called a hypnogogic state. In this state, you start getting woozy and feel your eyelids flutter. When you are in this state, say the following words—aloud—three times:

> I will remember my dreams clearly and well,
> and will record them when I wake up.

The phrasing of this suggestion is important, because it states that you will not just remember the dreams, but that you will record them as well. You can remember dreams in your belly (waking with butterflies in your stomach and not knowing why) and in your chest (waking with your heart racing). But you want to capture more than your body's memories. You want to capture your dream's *story*. When you make this suggestion aloud, saying it as specifically and clearly as possible, your brain takes your words at face value. By being specific and literal, you prepare your brain to remember.

What you hear in this state is immediately delivered as a message to your brain; in other words, it is self-hypnotic. Further, just as with hypnotic suggestion, because you are in an alpha state, you will be more willing to act on the direction. As we saw in chapter 2, once you start to fall asleep and move into the unconscious, you enter the theta phase. After that, you move into the delta phase, or deep sleep. Then you start cycling back again. Each time you dream, you complete a cycle that follows the shape of a wave. Naming your intentions aloud when you begin to enter the early phase of this cycle makes it much more likely that you will follow through. This process helped me to progress in a brief amount of time from recalling just a few dreams a year to nearly 200.

When you wake up, it is important that you record the date and whatever first comes into your awareness, no matter how insignificant it may seem. If all you remember is a green chair, just jot down "a green chair." Doing this even when you recall very little is still essential, because it "primes the pump," so to speak. Over the first few nights, you may wake and find you remember none or very little of your dreams. As you continue to practice the process, however, the memories of your dreams will begin to flow more easily. Your brain is often still in alpha phase when you first awaken, meaning that you remain in a somewhat hypnotic state. You may think you do not remember the specifics of your dream, but anything at all that comes to mind while you are in this state is still connected to your nighttime experience and your unconscious—so write it down.

Keep in mind as well that it truly does not matter if a dream seems to make no sense simply because it does not have the beauty or clarity of some of the examples provided in this book. Do not judge your dream. Observe it; embrace it; write it down. Observe and embrace the parts and the players; the message, characters, and colors; the sounds and feelings. Recall and record whatever you can. Remember that what you record now will be of use not only immediately, but throughout your life. When you record your dreams, you can consult that record whenever you feel the need to. Of the thousands of dreams I have recorded, there are very few I remember until I go back and reread my notes.

Here are some questions to consider as you record a dream:

* What are the particulars of the dream? What happened? Where were you? If the dream presents you with places and people you do not recognize, focusing on the feelings you experienced when you encountered them will help you later, as you begin your interpretation.

* Did you notice any smells? Smell is deeply connected to emotion because it is the single most powerful sense directly connected to the emotional center—the hypothalamus—in the brain.

* What emotions arose in your dream? It is important to note your emotions as you record, because the way you felt in the dream helps you to decipher its message and to refine the meaning of its images. For instance, imagine you dream of entering an empty house. Did you feel scared? Threatened? Excited? Welcome? Emotions provide context, so remember to note both how you felt in the dream and how you felt after you awoke. Whatever you feel when you awaken is another very good indicator of the dream's content and message.

* Were there other people in the dream? If so, how many and who were they?

* What was occurring in the dream when you woke up?

* If the dream is recurring, when did the dream begin and how long did you continue to have it?

* What did you feel while in the dream? Feeling will always provide a sense of the quality, or tone, of a dream. Consider whether you felt threatened, fearful, calm, relaxed, joyous, eager, or excited. Whatever feeling first comes into your awareness—for instance, feeling scared even though you may not remember anything frightening—trust it. Trust your unconscious, and then consider why, out of all possible feelings, you experienced the one you did.

Addressing these questions in closer detail later helps you to understand the dream's message and allows you to profit from the guidance it offers. You begin simply by noting exactly what your unconscious creates to get your attention.

Following this process just as I have described can dramatically improve your dream recall. I hear so often of people having vivid dreams that they remember perfectly the instant they wake up, whether in the middle of the night or in the morning. However—either because they have nothing nearby with which to record the dream, or because they assume they will remember it and put off jotting it down until morning—they do nothing. By the time they wake in the morning and start the day, even if they suddenly remember that they had intended to jot down last night's dream, they find that the memory of it is gone, even though it seemed so vivid just hours before.

If you wake up with the memory of a dream but, for whatever reason, cannot record it, try at least to speak the dream out loud. Tell your partner what you dreamed or, if you are alone, relate the dream aloud. I have found that the act of speaking helps a dream to stay with me better. As for anything you remember in the middle of the night, just try—really try—to write down whatever it is you recall at the moment. The truth is that, come morning, you are less likely to remember dreams experienced in the middle of the night, when you were likely in a deep, non-REM sleep. And waking suddenly from a deep sleep presents a rare opportunity to recall dreams from a phase of sleep in which they are rarely recalled.

Having a digital recording device by your bed makes this process very convenient. When you wake, no matter when, you can just grab it, press the button, and speak. It only takes a minute or two to record what you remember as you lie in bed. Just as if you were writing it down, give the date and quickly describe the dream. You can give it a title later, or even the next day. When you are recording, be very literal. Don't try to interpret; interpretation comes later, in steps 6 and 7.

With very detailed dreams, try not to get too bogged down in detail. Instead, consider what was most dramatic, or memorable, or out of place in the dream. For example, if you dream you are having dinner with your family, but there is an alligator sitting at the table, it is probably pretty important to note the alligator. It is actually the summary of the dream, rather than its full and completely detailed retelling, that best reveals its themes—hence, the importance of giving your dream a title. The next day, at your leisure, you can begin working your way through the other steps in the process. Now, all you want to do is to bring the dream up and out of your unconscious. Most of us lead very busy lives, so remember to keep it swift and simple.

If you are anxious to get started with this seven-step process or struggling to recall any elements of your dreams, you can use some of the illustrations and examples of dreams given in Part III, or else make up a dream, as described in chapters 13 and 17. The language of symbols is useful both within and outside of your dreams. No matter how you access it, however, remember that this language helps you better understand not just your dreams, but your waking life as well.

* * * * * * * * * * * * * * * * *

To sum up...

1. Place a voice recorder or notepad and pen within easy reach of your bed.

2. When you begin to feel you are drifting off to sleep, repeat aloud three times: "I will remember my dreams clearly and well, and will record them when I wake up."

3. When you awaken, whether in the morning or the middle of the night, quickly record whatever you can recall from your dream.

4. Be very literal. Jot down the first images and feelings that come to mind without judging or analyzing. Whatever comes to your mind, just note it and let it be.

CHAPTER 6

Step 2. Give Your Dream a Title

G iving your dream a title is a simple but very important step. Once you have practiced titling your dreams—instinctively, without trying to make sense of them or overthinking it—you will find that even the simplest titles give you insight into what each dream really means and guidance for working with it. Remember: A dream is like today's newspaper. When you glance at a newspaper, the headlines quickly summarize the stories within. Just by glancing at the front page, you get a sense of the contents. Your dreams' titles work in a similar way. One glance at the title gives you a sense, if not of the details or the full story, of what areas of your life the dream covers.

Unless you are a writer or a journalist, you probably don't have a lot of practice with giving things titles. If it feels a bit tricky at first, it may help if you begin by simply paying attention to newspaper headlines. As you read your morning newspaper or news website, as you pass by newspaper stands on your way to work, or as you idle over the magazine rack while grocery shopping, just take note of the headlines you see. Familiarizing yourself with how others approach titling things can give you an idea of how to come up with your own titles. Once you get the hang of it, the process will become instinctive to you and, thus, closer to your unconscious. Just remember always to go with the first thing that comes to mind.

When you give your dream a title, you begin the process of analyzing it. The key to analyzing your dreams is to keep things simple, especially when you are just beginning. Start with simply analyzing the title of the dream, exploring what it means both generally and personally. Consider the following dream titles, taken with permission from actual conversations with friends and clients:

* Lost and Found

* Possession

* The Bra

What might those words have indicated to the dreamers? What do they suggest to you? These titles are simultaneously simple and suggestive, because they were the first phrases that sprang to the dreamers' minds.

Sometimes the simplest phrases or images can be the most revealing. Don't worry if your dream seems too big for a single title. Some dreams are so detailed, covering so much time and ground, that you can get lost in the maze as you try to interpret them. Giving them a simple title like the ones above can help in these cases, because it helps you focus on the primary themes of your dream. The dreams corresponding to the titles noted above range from the very short and simple (a dream of a lacy bra) to the lengthy and complex (a full narrative involving a soul's departure from the body). In each case, the title helped the dreamer focus on the dream's most important details.

If you have trouble coming up with a title, try summarizing your dream and saying it aloud, very slowly. For instance: "I dreamed of a tall man climbing the stairs." Let the title come to you naturally. In this case, it could be as simple as "Climbing the Stairs" or "The Tall Man," or as abstract as "Ascension." The important thing is that your title be the first phrase or word that springs to your mind. This first impression will be the most revealing, the most useful, and, therefore, the most in tune with your unconscious.

Look at the three titles suggested above: "Climbing the Stairs," "The Tall Man," and "Ascension." Reread them, slowly. Each refers to the same content, yet each has a very different feeling and tone. "Climbing the Stairs" puts the focus on work, the effort it takes to go up. "The Tall Man" may imply an imposing figure or a representation of confidence, of standing tall. "Ascension" focuses entirely on the act of rising. As you can see, a title can provide important clues to a dream's meaning.

Consider this dream related in the Bible. Jacob dreamed of angels going up and down a ladder. In the dream, God told Jacob that he would one day bring Jacob and his descendants back to their homeland. The angels on the ladder were thus symbolic; the ladder symbolized a two-way street—climbing to heaven and reaching back down to earth—and the angels represented the powerful energy that emanates from faith. While people may not know the dream in detail, most people are very familiar with its title—"Jacob's Ladder." This simple title tells you so much about what is important in Jacob's dream and has resonated culturally for millennia.

So remember: Rather than struggling to come up with a title that makes sense logically or encapsulates all the elements of your dream, invite your unconscious into the work by always going with the first thing that comes to you. Once you have given your dream a title, repeat it aloud. Then, for the time being, acknowledge a job well done and set it aside.

* * * * * * * * * * * * * * * * *

To sum up...

1. Familiarize yourself with titling by paying attention to newspaper headlines and magazine story titles.

2. Let the title be the first word or phrase that comes to mind.

3. If you have trouble, try saying aloud a very basic summary of the dream's content to help identify its central themes.

4. Repeat your title aloud, slowly, and think about what the word or phrase means or suggests to you generally.

5. Set the dream and its title aside.

CHAPTER 7

Step 3. Read or Repeat Your Dream Aloud—Slowly

Dreams always reflect what is currently uppermost in your mind. Like a newspaper, they tell you something about the "current events" of your life. Remember this as you begin step 3, which is best done later in the day or, preferably, the day after the dream. Very slowly, reread or repeat aloud the dream as you have recorded it. When words are spoken too quickly, we often miss their essence. So when you speak your dream aloud, do it slowly. This slow meditation often proves surprisingly revealing and can begin to give you a better sense of what your dream is about. Just repeat the dream without interpretation, always keeping in mind that your dreams are always about you and you alone.

Have you ever dreamed of what seemed like a frightening situation? When you take the time to describe that situation slowly and steadily, you may find that the message revealed is encouraging and not at all frightening. A friend of mine told me she often dreamed of floods and drowning. I asked her to repeat her dream to me, slowly. When she slowed down, she had time to consider that, in the dream, she neither drowned nor feared drowning. Rather, she tried to stay afloat and always woke up before any harm came to her. By slowing down and reflecting, moment by moment, on what had actually happened in the dream, she was able to see that this dream, which at first seemed so alarming, was actually assuring her that, despite her inability to control all aspects of her life, she always found a way to stay afloat and ride out the flood—in this case, by waking up.

Another friend recalled a recurring dream from childhood in which she was falling through the air. She never knew exactly how she came to be falling; she was just suddenly falling through space. In the dream—and also while recollecting the dream—she felt panic. She described falling for what seemed like forever, as if she had been dropped out of the sky. She told me she prayed like crazy to wake up before she hit the ground. She remembered always waking from that dream with her heart racing and with a pounding in her chest. When I asked her to repeat the dream more slowly, we were able to come up with questions that revealed more about the dream's message.

I asked her whether it was day or night in the dream, and whether anyone was with her. She recalled that she had been falling in the daytime and that she had been alone in the dream. Symbolically, falling often represents something you cannot manage or control; you are out of control and cannot stop the fall without hurting yourself—that is, without hitting the ground. That was the essence of my friend's dream. She couldn't stop herself and instead fell farther and farther. As she slowly went over the details a second time, however, she felt noticeably less panicked and eventually realized that the dream offered a lovely message, which we put like this: You are falling; you are praying; and you never hit the bottom. Thus, your prayers will be answered. Your prayers will save you.

This is the beauty of dreams—even, as in this case, brief dreams with very few details. Some people may dismiss this dream as being "bad" or nonsensical, or not even bother to work with it, because dreams of falling are very common. Or perhaps they blame the feeling of falling on something they ate at dinner that upset their stomachs! But by pausing and speaking the dream slowly while considering every part of it, the meaning of the dream becomes clear—and in a highly personalized and supportive way that is applicable to waking life.

If you choose to discuss your dreams with another person or a group of people, remember that you must verbalize the description of your dreams yourself, even if your audience offers input and clarification. Imagine if, while my friend was describing her recurring dream of falling, I had said: "Well, of course you were afraid of hitting the ground—you would have died. But it's okay, because you woke up before that happened." If she accepted my analysis without verbalizing the facts of the dream, she probably wouldn't have found as much guidance in the dream as she did.

In fact, it helps immensely to repeat your dreams to yourself. In doing so, you acknowledge that you are the dreamer and thereby cross the bridge into your own unconscious. You use speech, language, to give information from your unconscious (the dream) to your left brain. When you do this slowly and for yourself, you are better able to notice the symbolic information that underlies the literal words. "I was falling from the sky and praying I would wake up before I hit the ground" becomes "When I feel out of control, praying or seeking support will save me." *I* may know what you mean; your *listener* (partner, friend, sibling) may know what you mean; but I want *you* to know what you mean—and to put that meaning into words.

You must always engage personally with your dreams, rather than letting someone else rush you through the process or provide meaning for you. Many years ago, I dreamed that I was descending a spiral staircase into a basement. I was moving quickly, gracefully, almost as if I were floating down the stairs. I was not falling; I was completely in control. Standard methods of interpretation might determine that this dream meant that I was losing something—that I was "descending" in life, and that the dream was a bad omen. I knew, however, that the dream had not been about "losing" anything from my life, because I had woken from it feeling thrilled, feeling exhilarated.

Remember, your response to a dream is often very telling when it comes to deciphering its message. So I ignored the standard interpretation of my dream, and considered it for myself. I repeated it aloud very slowly, while thinking about what else a basement could represent—and, most importantly, what a basement represented to me. Yes,

I thought, a basement is the lower part of a building, but it is also the only space in a home that resides within the earth, which makes it the deepest level of a home. This symbolic meaning resonated with me because, at the time in my life when I had the dream, I was increasingly committed to doing my own dreamwork and guiding other people to do the same. Thus, it became apparent that the dream was affirming for me that I was on the right path and that I was accessing deeper levels of my own unconscious. This illustrates why it is best to observe and embrace rather than judge.

Repetitive activities tend to help you access the unconscious, because the conscious brain becomes bored with repetitive tasks. You brush your teeth up and down; you wash the same dishes in the same sink; you take the same route home from work every day. Then one day, you seem to lose the time that elapses between beginning and completing the task, even though you have been awake the whole time. If you want to remain attentive to things that demand your focus—like driving—you have to vary the routine. Variation frees the conscious brain from boredom and forces it to be cognizant of your actions. When you slow down as you relate your dream, you force your brain to attend to its details.

Things always make sense if you look at them carefully. When you repeat your dream aloud, slowly—really listening and letting your left brain absorb what you are saying—you begin to translate your dreams *for yourself*. This is a key element of my simple method—to help you learn to interpret your dreams without relying on a dictionary, an analyst, or an interpreter. Your dreams will change substantially throughout your life, but what matters is *now*. You live in the present and need to see what is holding you back—see it, assess it, address it—so that you can move forward in your life immediately.

* * * * * * * * * * * * * * * * *

To sum up…

1. Repeat or reread your dream aloud.

2. Speak slowly, keeping in mind that the dreamer is always dreaming about the dreamer.

3. Verbalize your thoughts and feelings yourself, so that your brain fully absorbs the information. Don't let others do it for you.

CHAPTER 8

Step 4. Consider What Is Uppermost in Your Life Right Now

Once you have given your dream a title—a headline—you can approach it as if it were a corresponding news story. A newspaper reports on current events, today's events. But it also provides editorials. In the same way, your dreams will always address whatever is uppermost in your life right now and provide commentary on it, including suggestions for moving forward. If you are remembering older dreams, they will address both what is happening in your life now and what was happening in your life when you originally had the dream.

If you have ever heard other people discussing their own dreams, you may have noticed that they often wonder whether their dreams are prophetic—"I dreamed my mother died. Oh my god, it must mean she's going to die!" Dreams, however, do not typically foretell the future; rather, they clarify the present. For instance, a client recently dreamed of an explosion. She woke up terrified and convinced that the dream was a sign there would be an explosion in her house. When we began working on the dream, she was not convinced that the dream was only communicating symbolically. As people often do, she insisted: "Yes, it may have been symbolic, but it seemed so real."

After she had titled the dream—she quickly named it "Explosion"—and described it again—aloud and slowly—I asked her to tell me what was uppermost in her mind at the present moment. She said she had been under a lot of pressure at work, and that the stress of her workday was also manifesting in her interpersonal relationships. She had been arguing with her siblings and her partner, feeling as if no one appreciated the levels of stress she was experiencing. As she verbalized these issues, she was surprised to realize exactly how much anger and frustration she had been suppressing, both at work and when interacting with her loved ones. By clarifying and acknowledging what was truly on her mind, she came to understand that her dream was not a forewarning of literal explosion, but a warning that, if she continued to withhold and suppress all of that anger and frustration, she would flame out, or "explode," either at work or with her family.

Remember: The dreamer is always dreaming about the dreamer. Put simply, my client's dream was not about a literal explosion within her house, but a metaphorical explosion within *herself*. After all, at its most basic, a house is the space where we live our lives. Thus, the explosion in my client's dream indicates an explosion taking place, not in her physical house, but rather in her house as a symbolic emotional space in which she lives—her work, her family, her sexual relationships, her health, her body, her interactions with family and neighbors. When she understood this, she began to see the possibilities for guidance the dream offered. We will discuss this in more detail in step 7.

In fact, most dreams are not predictive, but rather related to whatever is currently going on in your life. And the relevant messages are often quite brief, no matter how long the dream may seem to run on. Indeed, as you begin to understand what your dreams are trying to tell you, they will likely grow shorter, as the unconscious can communicate more efficiently. Of course, there are times when the contents of a dream closely match major events that follow. For instance, people who dream of a tsunami before one strikes may exclaim: "Yes, I dreamed this would happen and saw this coming!" Well, that may be. However, before assuming a dream is prophetic or portentous, you must first take a careful look at what is going on in your daily life to make sure that your dreams guide you toward constructive ends, rather than inducing fear.

In this case, a tsunami is a powerful and sudden force that overwhelms those in its path. Therefore, if you dream of a tsunami, it may be useful to consider what powerful forces in your life threaten to overwhelm you with waves of emotion. These "forces" may be feelings, relationships, or situations. Remember, your dreams will always address whatever is uppermost in your life, and what is truly uppermost in your life will usually be what comes to mind first. What uncontrollable events are occurring in your life? Or what do you fear may occur in your life that will make you feel as if you are being swept away, drowned?

When you approach your dreams in this way, you can see dreams of impending disaster not as prediction or prophecy, but as urgent messages from your unconscious: "Wake up! Something in your life is threatening to overwhelm you!" Once you identify what those forces or situations are, you can prepare for them and deal with them before you are overwhelmed. These preparations are far more useful for making progress in your daily life than fears of impending and external disasters, over which you truly have no immediate control.

In step 4, simply consider your front-page headlines. What is uppermost in your present, waking life—right now? It does not matter how great or small those things may be. If what is most relevant to you is that you just had a huge fight with your daughter or an argument with your spouse, then that is probably what is uppermost in your life. If you then dream of guns, ask yourself if you are feeling inept in the face of your own anger. Are you feeling so angry that you want to lash out? Are you afraid of using or abusing your power against the people you love? Whatever is going on in your present, waking life is what will be reflected in the dream.

If you are having trouble coming up with examples from your own experience, begin by considering what is happening at home, at work, or in your relationships. Be instinctive and work with the first thing or two that comes to mind. You have already given your dream a title and slowly repeated it aloud. Now determine what is actually on your mind and your dream's symbols will begin to fall into place.

* * * * * * * * * * * * * * * * * *

To sum up...

1. Quickly review the title and/or summary of the dream with which you are working.

2. Assess what is uppermost in your life right now, looking carefully at your work, your family, your relationships, etc.

3. Be instinctive. Whatever first comes to your mind is most likely what your dream addresses.

CHAPTER 9

Step 5. Describe Your Dream as if Talking to a Martian

Our attempts to understand everything in terms of logic is, ironically, a major reason why we are so confused and overwhelmed when we try to comprehend our dreams. It is also why people live with the illusion that it is incredibly difficult to make sense of their lives. It is not. The key is to look at your life without judgment. In this book, you are learning the language of dreams because that language is so rich. However, the value of learning the language of the unconscious is that it can take you beyond just understanding your dreams and help you understand who you are and who you can be. Why? Because our higher selves and the Divine also speak to us through the language of symbols and dreams.

After you have recorded your dream, named it, slowly repeated it aloud, and considered what is uppermost in your life, it is time to begin describing the elements of the dream. Do this as if you were talking to a Martian. For instance, say you recorded the following dream: "I was sitting in a beautiful armchair and it felt so comfortable." If you tell this to a Martian, he will likely have no idea what an armchair is. So how do you describe an armchair? Think in terms of both its function and what it represents. If you tell a Martian that you are "falling from very high in the sky," you may have to explain that falling from "very high" is extremely dangerous, extremely frightening, because it indicates that you are quite far away from the ground. Thus, you are more likely to get hurt than if you were to fall off, for instance, that armchair.

This may feel a little strange at first—which is, of course, the point—but a picture is worth a thousand words. When you begin to describe what seems blatantly obvious to you—in painstaking detail, using very simple words—you access more of your dream's intentions more clearly. Each dream image can contain so much information, and the best way to unspool that information in the left brain is to verbalize the image in all its facets and complexity. Most of us, of course, lack the time and the will to sit there and interpret each image in a thousand words. And remember that an essential aspect of this process is to complete it swiftly and simply. Despite what we often believe, it is sometimes by making a process quick and easy that we make it more deeply effective.

So how do you know which details to explain to our hypothetical Martian? This is something best taught through illustration and learned through practice. For instance, one of my clients—we'll call her "C"—recalled a recurring dream from childhood. The narrative of the dream primarily concerned navigating a maze. She titled this dream "The Maze" and, when it came time to break it into its interpretive parts, she and I ("DEC" below) shared the following exchange:

C: In the dream, I am at home, walking through a maze. It's fun; it feels safe; and I'm enjoying it.

DEC: Let's begin there, then. If I don't know what a maze is, how do you define it?

C: A maze is a series of passageways or dead ends. You follow a path that goes in many directions, zigzagging your way through.

A maze is enclosed, so if you get lost you have to turn around and try another route.

DEC: How do you describe the goal of working a maze to someone who never heard of mazes?

C: The goal is to travel the various routes until you are able to find your way from A to Z.

By breaking the dream down into its disparate parts and describing them in the most basic way possible—as if to someone with no experience with anything she was talking about—my client learned that the dream was illustrating the many challenges she would experience going from start to finish. From then to now; from the beginning of life to its end. It was telling her that, although there may be a lot of zigzagging and a few wrong turns in life, her time here is an adventure and she has many options to try.

Of course, if you dream of being chased through a dark, claustrophobic maze late at night, the meaning may be very different. In that case, the maze may indicate something in which you feel pursued and trapped, most likely associated with a situation causing you anxiety in your waking life. This is a perfect illustration of why dream dictionaries just do not work. A topiary maze explored and enjoyed on a beautiful, bright day is obviously very different from a haunted maze in a horror film! Your interpretation needs to be useful to *you*. Taking the time to belabor the obvious is an important step toward understanding the layers of symbolic meaning within each image from your dreams.

Focus on the Details

As you begin to interpret your own dreams, you may find them crammed with details, and may have difficulty knowing where to focus. First, remember that the whole point is to keep it easy and simple. When you begin by describing everything in the simplest terms possible, complex symbols and images begin to make sense and to fall into place. As always, the more you practice, the easier it gets. Practice really is key.

Once you get used to describing things so simply that even a Martian can understand them, it becomes habit. Explaining images to someone who doesn't understand them always brings up clues, especially if the image, or dream, is very complex. This is important to remember when you are working with a longer, more detailed, meandering dream. You do not have to interpret every little detail, just what is most dramatic.

Recently, a friend ("E") had what he initially described as an "insignificant" dream that he believed was simply about his daytime job. In the dream, he arrived at work and found the foreman's wallet lying on the floor. We began there:

DEC: Tell me, what is a foreman? Explain it in the simplest way possible—as if you were talking to a Martian.

E: A foreman is the man who runs a crew of people working on the floor.

DEC: So, someone in charge. What is a wallet?

E: A wallet is something you carry with you to hold your money.

DEC: Is that all you carry in a wallet? Just your money?

E: Well, it holds your money and things like your driver's license, IDs, pictures, and personal items.

DEC: Ah, so this dream is not necessarily about money; it is about a wallet—a place where you store personal things, like your ID and pictures. What is a picture?

E: A picture is a photograph of a person.

DEC: And what is a photograph?

E: A photograph is a record or an image of a person.

DEC: An image of just anyone?

E: Well, no.

DEC: Okay, then, who appears in the pictures you carry in your wallet?

E: My family.

DEC: And what does family mean?

E: My family is the people I love: my wife, my kids, my dog.

DEC: Who are your wife, your kids, and your dog?

E: They are the people and beings most important to me.

DEC: Okay. Let's look at this dream again, now that we have discussed and explored the essence and meaning of its details—the foreman, the wallet, etc. Repeat your dream.

E: I arrive at the place where I work. There, I find an object that contains the identification, recorded images of loved ones, and money of someone in charge.

DEC: Perfect. Now think about what you have just said in terms of its relevance to what is currently uppermost on your mind in your waking life.

E: Well, at home and at work, I feel I have been losing a lot of control and not taking any back for myself. Maybe I need to find a way to be more like a foreman, like someone in charge.

DEC: And you have dropped—or lost—the identity of the one in control. Considering this, what is the message, the importance, of the dream?

E: Actually, I think it is showing me that I need to relocate my sense of authority by taking back some control. When I find that authority and control again—control over my identity, or my life and my decisions—I will also find that it strengthens my life in terms of my finances, my relationships with my family, and my sense of self.

DEC: Absolutely! This dream is a message from your unconscious saying that you have lost touch with the decisive part of your identity and suggesting that you find a way to take back some control. It is saying that you can maintain your career, your finances, your relationships with your family—that is, find them again and carry them with you—if you take control of your life and act decisively.

Even if your dream does not present you with a narrative as clear as the one I have just described, it still contains plenty of information with which you can begin to work. If all you dream is that you are in your bedroom, describe what a bedroom is. That is, a bedroom is not only a place to sleep; it is also a private place, often a safe place, a place where you make love and rest. Or perhaps you dream of a sofa. How do you describe a sofa to a Martian? As a piece of furniture on which you sit or rest. But an equally important aspect of a sofa is that it is usually a place where you sit with other people. What about a bathroom? A bathroom is where you wash and clean yourself or use the toilet. What is a toilet? A toilet is a vessel into which you release and discharge waste materials and toxins. In waking life, those waste materials and toxins are physical. But, if you are working with a dream, they may just as easily be emotional.

Digging Deeper

When you explore multiple facets of an object, you access ever-deeper levels of meaning. Let's try another example. You dream about being in the kitchen. What is a kitchen? A kitchen is a room in a home. What do you do there? You store and prepare food, and maybe also consume it. Basically, a kitchen is associated with food. And what is food? Food is nourishment. Nutrients. Food is something you need; without it, you die. Food is the essence of life and represents nourishment not just in terms of nutrition, but in terms of nurture, or love, as well.

If you dream of standing in a kitchen and everything is a horrible mess—trash bin overflowing, dishes stacked to the ceiling—it may surprise you if you are very tidy and neat in waking life. How you are in waking life, however, is not the point, because what is the dream saying? Simply put, it is a chaotic mess in the space in your life that provides physical and/or emotional nourishment. That is, the mess may concern food directly (what you eat in your waking life), but what about the next level of meaning? What about nurture and love? This dream may be saying that the situations in your life upon which you depend for nourishment and love are a mess. In other words, your emotional life is in disarray. Remember, even simple dreams offer valuable information, because their message is very concentrated.

Consider the symbol of a gun. I have a client who was a sharpshooter in the army and became a gun hobbyist. If she were to dream about a gun, it would have a great deal of symbolic relevance. She enjoys guns and knows how to handle and manage them, but they also have direct relevance to what she has achieved in her life. For me, guns are foreign objects, scary instruments of which I have no knowledge. When it comes to dreams, however, the objective reality of a gun is not the point. The point is the subjective relationship between the individual and the object that inhabits his or her dreams.

If I describe a gun to a Martian, I probably describe it as an instrument of killing and death. If, on the other hand, my client describes the same object, she likely describes it as an instrument of skill that can be used to attack, defend, or, in the case of hunting, feed your family. Whatever the object represents in *your* life is what it means in *your* dream, *your* unconscious. Because you are the one entering the unconscious, the symbolic import of the images that appear to you there will always involve the aspects most relevant to you. When you are defining elements of your dreams, it is vital that you listen to your own definition, because each person's description will be totally different.

Common Symbols

That said, it is worthwhile to note that there are symbols that are so very common and that so frequently mean the same things to so many people that they can almost be considered universal. For instance, for many of us, the ocean represents emotion, its salty and life-giving fluid similar to the state in which the fetus resides while it develops. As humans, we are 75 percent water. Water is therefore the essence of life, the continuation of life, and the expression of life, all of which have to do with emotion as well. Still, if you dream that you are swimming easily among gentle waves of clear, blue water, it probably demonstrates that your unconscious and your emotions are very clear to you. If, on the other hand, you are being battered by choppy waves of murky, cold water, it may indicate that you are suspended in an emotional state in which you are unable to understand clearly the influence of your unconscious.

Some other common symbols include cars, brakes, purses, and wallets. Let's describe each to our Martian. What is a car? It is a vehicle that carries you from point A to point B. Similarly, the body is the vehicle that carries your soul from the beginning of life to its end. What are brakes? They are designed to control the speed of a vehicle and to bring it to a stop. If, then, you dream that you are driving and the brakes on your car fail, it may relate to an area in your waking life where you have lost, or are simply choosing not to exert, control. For instance, if you are struggling with poor nutrition, it may be that your dream is showing you that you are not exerting control over your body and health.

As detailed in the dream of the lost wallet described above, purses and wallets—objects in which you carry money, identification, and personal effects—are closely related to identity, particularly in terms of your finances, your sense of self, and your relationships. And what does money mean when it appears in a dream? Money is a form of currency, something you use to acquire things. Like money, knowledge or blessings are also means to acquiring things, particularly things less tangible. Money is energy, exchange—payment for a service or something as tangible as a shirt or a car. It facilitates the connection of trade, of people moving forward comfortably in their lives—comfortably in the material world, that is, because of course you cannot take material possessions with you into the next life.

If you dream of seasonal landscapes, consider your feelings about each. Describe the colors and fragrances, which always correspond to emotions and feelings. If the land is full and lush, you are dreaming of summer, the season of growth; you are growing in your life. Thick vegetation, trees in full bloom with green leaves and flowers, are among the natural things that keep you alive. If the landscape is not yet thriving, but is budding and new, you are probably dreaming about spring, the season of new beginnings. If the trees have variously colored bright leaves and the scent of pumpkin is in the air, you are dreaming of autumn, a time of harvest and preparation. And though it represents the end of the year for us, a snowy landscape covered in frost does not necessarily mean the end of life or of anything else. Winter is a time of rest, a time to stay warm indoors and, for many, a time to celebrate various holidays. As you can see, even the settings of your dreams can reveal much about the messages they contain from your unconscious.

Another common subject of dreams is a mother. Regardless of the quality of your relationship with your mother, she is the single most important person in your life because you were carried inside of her for nine months. During that time, whatever she ate, felt, or experienced, you ate, felt, and experienced. As infants, we have no sense of being separated from our mothers even after the umbilical cord is cut. For the first few years, we have no sense of self as separate from our mothers. Understanding the meaning of this relationship generally helps you understand what it means when your own mother appears in your dreams. By digging deeper and considering what your mother, or motherhood itself, means to you, you can further illuminate a dream's message.

In a similar way, people often dream that they are visited by the deceased after someone they love has died. Some may believe, or wish to believe, that these dreams are visions, visitations from the dead. But the important question to ask when this happens is not whether the dream is "real," but rather what the deceased represented in your life. For instance, after my aunt passed, I dreamed that she and I were together. As glad as I was to see her again, I thought about what she had meant to me. My aunt had been a kind and caring person, but was also very passive. When she felt strong emotions and wanted to talk about them, other people in her life often discouraged her from doing so, and she went along with it. Thus, my dream of my aunt led me to ask myself: Where in my life am I perhaps being too kind and not assertive enough to take care of and express myself? This questioning helped me clarify unhealthy situations in my waking life.

Even if you dream that a departed loved one has returned to give you advice or caution, the message still comes from you, and is about you. That is, the dream is actually concerned not with your desire to reconnect with those who have passed away, but with what those people represented to you. The dream is still about your story when you are awake and—whether or not it is a vision or a visitation—the response and outcome are still the same.

Many people are able to fly in their dreams. Let's work with that. Flying is soaring, freedom, rising above everyday things. But it also represents something that is not possible for human beings. Gravity holds us to the earth. So when you rise above gravity and soar, you transcend the limitations of being human and rise above your own issues. As you begin to soar, your unconscious may be telling you: "Yes, you can! You can do the impossible; you can rise above it all!" Thus, when you fly in a dream, you not only soar above the everyday world; you transcend limitations.

Moreover, when you soar above the conscious world, you gain a different perspective on it—a much wider, fuller view of what lies below you. The vast majority of the time, flying dreams are delightful, not traumatic. A friend who frequently dreams of flying once told me something illuminating. In her dreams, when she wants to fly, she simply takes a deep breath and that is what allows her to rise into the air. This is significant, because it represents such a clear message from the unconscious. By taking a deep breath—that is, by remaining balanced and calm—she can rise above the problems and concerns of the conscious world. She further described how, when faced with a threat or burden in her flying dreams, she begins to feel heavy and starts to descend. When this happens, if she simply relaxes and takes another deep breath, she begins to rise again. Her unconscious is affirming for her that, as long as she remains calm and relaxed, she can rise above her burdens.

Negative Symbols

The existence of threats or burdens in dreams is an important symbol in and of itself—although not necessarily a negative one. The truth is that, as humans, we will always have problems and challenges with which to contend in our conscious lives. In my friend's case, her dream of flying, rather than warning of problems, was actually preparing her to meet those challenges when they inevitably arise. She just needs to remember that all she has to do is to remain calm so that she can transcend them.

Another example of a symbol that is often considered negative or frightening, but need not necessarily be so, is fire. Fires can, of course, be very frightening and overwhelming. Left unchecked, a raging fire can destroy everything from a home, to a city, to an entire forest. However, fire is also a means of purification. In purification by fire, you allow yourself to be consumed symbolically by something totally overwhelming, so that you can emerge from it healed, cleansed, and aware. The story of the phoenix, who is consumed by flames only to be reborn from its own ashes, is a beautiful example of this notion. If you dream of fire, work through steps 1 through 4 and then begin describing fire to a Martian. Whatever elements of fire seem most relevant to you will help you to understand what the fire in your dream indicates.

Other symbols that frighten and concern people are wild animals— snakes in particular. When people dream of snakes, they usually think it is a bad omen. Some dream dictionaries even claim that the appearance of a snake in a dream indicates that someone is envious of you and wishes you harm. How useful is it, however, to go through life wondering who wishes to hurt you out of spite or envy? In fact, snakes represent something beyond external envy. A snake is a cold-blooded creature with no limbs. It sheds its skin and is sometimes venomous, which means it can bite and inject a substance into its victim that is very harmful and sometimes fatal. Fear of snakes is found across many countries and cultures. But why are snakes so frightening to so many people?

Snakes blend into the environment, which means they can go unseen. They slither; they can move silently. If you are resting in a cave, you may not hear a snake coming. If you are in a field or savannah, you may not see a snake coiled in the grasses. If you are in the desert or mountains, you may not see a snake hiding beneath a rock. If you are up in the branches of a tree, an alligator may have trouble reaching you, but not a snake. The fear of snakes, then, is likely so prevalent because snakes represent a silent, unknowable threat. No matter your environment or level of awareness, a snake can harm you.

But snakes also transform; they shed their old skins and renew themselves. Thus, a snake can also represent transformation. This is one reason why the caduceus—the staff carried by Hermes that represented alchemy or transformation in ancient traditions and is now more commonly recognized as the symbol for medicine and physicians—features two snakes entwined around a staff. For some, the caduceus represents sexuality. Freud would see it as representing a phallus. This is yet another illustration of how our symbols are perfectly adapted to us as individuals. For most, snakes represent a silent threat. For others, they represent something beautiful and fascinating.

Snakes are multidimensional in their symbolism and are a common symbol in dreams. If you only perceive them as a threat, you may miss out on their multifaceted nature. Imagine you dream that a snake suddenly appears in your lap, and you jump up, terrified, to hurl it away from your body. If you wake up and nourish that fear by assuming the snake was a bad omen or banish it from your mind, you may miss out on important information it carried as a dream symbol. What are you trying to avoid in your waking life that is sneaking up on you silently? Sexuality? Healing or change? Accessing the unconscious? Is there a part of your life or yourself that is experiencing transformation, a shedding of the old to reveal the new?

Describing your dream as if talking to a Martian may seem odd or unwieldy at first. With just a little bit of practice, however, this process becomes a natural habit—something you can do anywhere and anytime. This imagined dialog can become an entertaining and essential part of your mastering the language of symbols. It can help you understand your dreams better, and also advance your fluency in the language of symbols as they occur in other areas of your life—in your spiritual practice, in your artwork, and in the events that make up your everyday waking world.

* * * * * * * * * * * * * * * * *

To sum up...

1. Consider which details stand out the most in your dream.

2. Describe those details as if talking to a Martian, or someone with absolutely no shared frame of reference.

3. Belabor the obvious. If something seems to go without saying, say it anyway. Explaining the obvious aloud offers clues to a dream's meaning.

4. Think about symbols that commonly occur in your dreams and familiarize yourself with their meaning and intent. This helps you to interpret dreams more quickly and easily as you move forward.

CHAPTER 10

Step 6. Summarize the Message from Your Unconscious

I n the 1990s, I had what seemed like a troubling dream. I dreamed that I had contracted the ebola virus, which, in my waking life, had been receiving a lot of media attention. The frightening and often-fatal virus seemed to have originated in Africa; most people who contracted it died within a matter of hours. The essential qualities of the illness and the atmosphere in which I dreamed that I had contracted it are central to my understanding of the dream. As portrayed in the media, those who contracted ebola typically perished from massive blood loss; their blood vessels deteriorated and burst causing massive hemorrhaging. Apparently, neither doctors nor epidemiologists understood how the virus spread, but it seemed to be spreading rapidly.

At first glance, this dream may seem alarming. But the remarkable aspect of the dream was that, in it, I lived. Not only did I survive the virus; I regained my health. To understand this dream, I put its story into a few simple sentences to convey what the unconscious was really saying. I first considered that the ebola virus represented a horrible death, total vulnerability, and something for which there was no known cure. But the dream showed me that, even if I had to endure terrifying experiences, I could survive them and heal. The basic message of the dream was this: If I can overcome something as awful as the ebola virus and recover from it, I can manage and recover from the pressures of my waking life.

And this is the essence of step 6: Sum up the message from your unconscious. In other words, what is your unconscious telling you in the dream? If, for instance, you dream that you are living in a very small and cramped space, what is your unconscious saying related to your current waking life? Use common sense in your approach and do not overthink the message; do not let your left brain take over. Don't be too literal and respond by thinking about how large or small your actual house is in waking life. Remember: The dream is not literal. Dreaming that you live in a claustrophobic space may be the dream's way of alerting you to the fact that you feel cramped in your life, that you lack the space and time you need. Your house in your dream may represent a relationship, your career, your ideas or ways of thinking, or other "spaces" into which you feel crammed. Your dream simply chose to represent these "spaces" in your life as a house, because, considered symbolically, a house is where most of us live our lives.

Summarizing a message from the unconscious can be awkward at first, but be patient with yourself. Any seeming lack of clarity stems from the fact that these messages are given to you in a new language— the language of symbols, of the right brain, of the unconscious. When you try to understand these messages with your left brain, you tend to take them literally. This is why we interpret dreams of disaster simply as warnings of impending threats. But this forecloses the possibilities for insight and guidance that these dreams offer us. Our familiarity with (and tendency to favor) left-brain interpretations can misdirect our efforts. We try to use literal methods to understand the innately nonliteral messages of the unconscious, when what we should be doing is learning, practicing, and mastering the language of symbols. Remember, in the left brain, 1 + 1 is always and can only ever be 2; in the right brain, 1 + 1 is merely a suggestion for myriad possibilities.

Understanding and embracing these possibilities is the essential lesson of dream interpretation. Each night, your unconscious speaks in your dreams and offers you amazing, useful advice that, if understood and acted upon, can and will improve your life—quickly. But these messages cannot be accessed through the logical left brain; to access them, you must learn the language of the symbolic right brain. If things do not seem to make sense to your waking mind, you can discover the meaning of them by increasing the fluidity with which you move between your conscious and unconscious worlds. This is how you learn to access more effectively the 95 percent of your brain's functioning that occurs in the unconscious.

Dream Warnings

Because stories are often our best teachers, I will share numerous dreams—some my own, others from friends and colleagues—as a means of explaining step 6. We have already seen how dreams that may seem predictive can still be relevant to your current waking life. One remarkable illustration of this is a dream experienced by a physician living in Israel who dreamed that he was out in the desert, wearing a soldier's uniform and standing with the army. When he awoke, he first assumed—correctly, as it turned out—that the dream was predictive and told his wife that they would be going to war again. What is interesting about this particular dream, however, is that this knowledge did not frighten him; he was able to accept it and prepare himself accordingly. Thus the dream was useful not just as a prediction, but as direction for his waking life.

At the time this man experienced his dream, he was deeply unhappy in his marital relationship. In the dream, he saw a desert—an arid landscape without the ability to nourish flowers or trees—and a war—a symbol of conflict. Thus, while the dream was predictive on one level—war, in fact, did come—it was also a symbolic representation of the conflict that he was enduring in his primary relationship, and a warning that the relationship was not nourishing to his soul. While the occurrence of a war may seem to corroborate his assumption that the dream was predictive, that can only ever be speculation. What is not debatable is that the dream reflected symbolically the actual situations that composed his daily, waking life.

Here's another example. Recently, my friend's daughter began repeatedly dreaming that her partner was cheating on her. When she woke up from these dreams, she was practically paralyzed, because she could not accept this possibility emotionally. Her partner was always incredibly supportive and deeply loyal to her. In waking life, she never doubted his fidelity. But, in fact, the dream had nothing to do with her partner. Rather, it was an anxiety dream in which her partner—who represented the most reliable and dependable figure in her life—failed her, leaving her lonely and vulnerable. Therefore, the useful question becomes: Where in waking life was she feeling unstable, lonely, and vulnerable?

Make no mistake about it: Questions like this can be very difficult to address. Facing a frightening or upsetting dream and, more important, facing the issues the dream represents can be very intimidating when you are awake. That is why it is important to let the dream sit for a while before you begin to interpret it. Don't try to work with a dream as soon as you wake up; come back to it later, when you are calm. When you awaken from a scary or upsetting dream, your limbic system has been setting off fireworks. You are in fight-or-flight mode; your heart is racing; your muscles are contracted; anxiety and fear are overwhelming you. You have to calm down before you do the dreamwork in order to access the upper regions of your brain. Feeling fear is okay; but moving beyond it is important.

The dream of my friend's daughter seems to indicate that there is something going on in her waking life that makes her feel threatened by instability. In fact, she had recently been fired from a job for repeated tardiness, despite several warnings. She had started a new job, but the dream continued, probably because she was not paying attention to some of the behaviors that had led to her past trauma. These same behaviors, because she continued to ignore them, still persisted as patterns in her waking life. The only way to stop them was to claim responsibility for them. Finding a new job made her feel better temporarily, but what she really needed to do was to face the qualities within herself that needed to be changed so that she could create different outcomes. Her dream was advising her that it was of the utmost importance to begin working toward prevention immediately. Her recurring dream—a repeated message from her unconscious—was urging her to do something about her behavior so that she would not have to keep repeating stressful, destabilizing experiences.

Nightmares

Nightmares, in and of themselves, can seem like stressful, destabilizing experiences. This is why sometimes, when we wake up from nightmares, we do not want to look too closely at them. We may not even want to go back to sleep, because we are afraid we may slip back into the nightmare. This is because nothing terrifies us more than looking closely at ourselves, and nightmares often deal with some aspect of ourselves or our lives that we resolutely do not wish to confront. You must remember, however, that as long as you do not answer the door, your dreams will just knock louder and more persistently. If you answer, if you receive the message, you can ease the fear of the nightmare returning.

A friend of mine told me of a recurring nightmare from which she awoke sweating, her heart racing, afraid even to get out of bed. In the dream, she had the sensation of leaving her body and soaring through her house. During her journey, she saw frightening shadows and heard demonic, maniacal laughter. She titled the dream "Witchcraft." Next, we talked to the Martian. What is witchcraft? It is a way of controlling the environment, the body, or sometimes people. Upon further discussion, my friend was able to get to the essence of the message from her unconscious. She feared being controlled by exterior forces—for instance, a troubled economy—but she also felt that she was too controlling of others. This was difficult for her to acknowledge, but once she did, she was able to take steps to face her fears (declaring bankruptcy, setting a stricter budget), which also helped her to be more comfortable relinquishing some of the control she had been trying to exert over her partner. Sure enough, her stress level decreased and the dream stopped.

In another example, a friend recalled a nightmare she had been having since early childhood. She dreamed she was lying in bed and needed desperately to get to an emergency exit nearby. However, she could not seem to get out of bed, no matter how hard she tried. Every time she tried to get up and go to the door, she felt shoved back down in her bed. She titled the dream "Panic." And, as it turned out, this simple, one-word title was the key to unlocking its message.

Panic is the experience of being mortally terrified, to the point of losing control over your body and mind. It is fear in its rawest form. Because this dream had continued throughout so much of her life, I asked my friend to describe the current events in her life at the time she began having the dream and then to consider her current state of mind. Looking back, she recalled feeling afraid all the time. Her father drank heavily and was often violent, so there was constant conflict in her life. As she dug deeper into the symbols in her dream, she came to understand that the door represented a way to escape her childhood fears—an "emergency exit," or a route of egress in the event of catastrophe. For a vulnerable child, the most likely means of escape were probably disassociation or death. The fact that she was unable to get to the door, however, was a symbolic way for her unconscious to convey that her soul was keeping her where she was because it was not yet her time to leave.

When we are very young, we do not often consider that our decisions are the result of free choice. We think of free choice as a privilege reserved for adults who can make decisions about their own lives and experiences. But children have free choice as well. They just don't know how to express that freedom yet. In fact, it usually gets expressed in the unconscious, generally in very vivid dreams. These dreams, which can seem so frightening, are often relaying important and supportive messages. In the dream described above, the message was this: As much as routes of escape may seem appealing, it is important to survive, to remain connected to life, and to endure. Of course, this is not an easy thing to face.

Memories and fears experienced in childhood are often so vivid that they can affect us well into adulthood. Maintaining your own sense of safety is important, so when you become upset or fearful while addressing a dream, pause and consider what the dream is triggering and counter it with your present experiences, reminding yourself that you are safe right now and will be okay. For instance, when I noticed my friend's anxiety, I reminded her and assured her that she was safe now. Then our conversation turned to our intense gratitude for being where we were in our lives at that moment—how wonderful it was to be fifty and not five, and to be safe in our own homes surrounded by love and support, totally empowered in life. By verbalizing, naming, and facing fears that you encounter in your dreams, you can keep those fears—and those recurring dreams—from returning, because, once you face the fear, the dream will have fulfilled its task.

Two of my own recurring dreams illustrate this. In the first, I dreamed I had lost something important to me—my purse, my date-book; there were slight variations, but the premise was always the same. When I noticed I had lost the item, I became extremely anxious. Despite seeming fairly innocuous, this dream was a nightmare, one from which I awakened relieved. In one version, I dreamed that I lost my appointment book. At that time, I was a practicing therapist and losing my appointment book would have been a disaster. All of my work, my appointments, my very existence was contained in that book. In another version, I lost my patient files. These contained not only my professional information and notes, but also confidential information my patients had entrusted to me. Each occurrence of the dream was a slightly different version of the same story, each time communicating something that I had not yet discerned. Finally, after I had started to practice my dreamwork, I had the following version of the dream. I entered a store and laid down my purse to pay with a credit card. When I returned to my car, I realized I did not have my purse. As I began to panic, I woke up.

The next day, I titled the dream "I Lost My Purse." I slowly repeated the dream and the title aloud, thinking about what was going on in my life. At a time when many of my colleagues were retiring, I had decided to transition from being a full-time clinical therapist to doing readings and dreamwork. Of course, there was anxiety attached to that decision. Next, describing aspects of the dream to my Martian friend, I defined a purse as a bag in which women carry personal items related to money and identity. By the time I arrived at step 6, I could see that the dream was showing me how, in waking life, I was experiencing intense fear—fear that I would lose my identity as a therapist as well as suffer financially. As is so often the case, once I recognized and understood those fears, I was able to confront them, allay them, and move past them.

The other recurring dream was very pleasant, and changed gradually over time. In early versions of the dream, I looked on the ground and found a few pennies. When I bent down to collect them, I found more and more pennies. Each time, I had to bend down to the ground, which is a gesture of humility, but also represents having to work to retrieve a reward. The reassurance the dream was offering me was this: There will always be more than you think, no matter what anxieties you have about money. There will always be enough, but you need to do your part and work in order to seek, find, and retrieve it.

Over the years, my dream continued and the value of the coins began to increase, until, finally, I dreamed that, rather than coins, I found a diamond ring on the floor. This time, when I bent down for it, instead of more coins, I found more diamonds, rubies, and precious stones. In other words, the dream was conveying that not only would I have enough to make ends meet; I would also have riches. Then I did not have the dream again for two decades. When it did recur, it was once more a ring that I found on the floor. In this version, however, as soon as I picked up the ring, the diamonds began to transform, growing larger and larger before turning into white, and then pink, crystals. As I gathered them, there were suddenly more and more crystals.

Then, for the first time in this dream, other people appeared nearby and I encouraged them to pick up the rest of the crystals. And so the "riches" were transformed into ancient vehicles of light and spirituality that take hundreds of thousands of years to form—crystals—that I could share with other people. This time, the dream was demonstrating the potential not only for material gain, but for progress on my spiritual journey. Through the transformation and my sharing the transformed objects with others, the dream assured me that I would get what I wanted and needed in terms of spiritual knowledge, and there would be so much of it that I could share it with others. In my case, that sharing is achieved through my books.

Practical Dreams

Messages from the unconscious, however, can also be extremely practical. Nearly thirty years ago, I was faced with making an important decision about a relationship I had with a man with whom I had many things in common. We were both divorced, both held doctorates, and both wanted to remarry and start a family. In other words, we seemed like a perfect fit. Still, though he kept asking me to commit to him, I found myself hedging, saying that I wasn't sure, and that we should just wait and see. It seemed odd to me that, despite our complementary "resumés," I was so very uncertain about accepting his proposal.

As I was struggling with that decision, I dreamed I was walking down a city street. As I walked, I passed a newsstand that was selling my "autobiography"—as written by someone else! Because the very notion of this was preposterous—it was the alligator at the dinner table—I recognized it immediately as a vital detail. This was my unconscious very clearly saying: "This is your story, but you are letting others write it, so pay attention." In the dream, I purchased the book and read it as I continued down the street. Suddenly, I snapped the book shut and said aloud: "This is not my story. I do not like the way it ends." That was it, start to finish. When I woke up in the morning, I finally knew exactly what I needed to do. I needed to end the romantic relationship that was the uppermost concern in my life at the time. My decision may sound dramatic, but the message from my dream was so clear, definitive, and specific.

The dream clearly showed me reading my own story and snapping the book shut, disowning it. When I applied this to my waking life, I realized that the most important situation in my life was my relationship with this man and my decision whether or not to marry him. Moreover, it had been bothering me that I was feeling so unsure, even though, when approached from a practical, logical point of view, the marriage seemed to make so much sense. We shared a spiritual history (we were both Jewish), an educational history, myriad interests, and a desire for a family. And it was evident that he was crazy about me. Despite all of the logical arguments for continuing the relationship, however, the dream's message was clear. I had to end it immediately because, if it were to continue, I would not like the way my own story ended. This was a warning dream. And I never regretted or doubted my decision.

Months later, I heard that the man had a very serious problem with alcohol. Even though I had been a therapist for years, I had not recognized the clear indications of alcoholism in my own personal relationship. My unconscious, however, was paying attention. It recognized that his drinking was problematic and sent me a dream to warn me that, if I continued on the path I was considering, I would allow exterior circumstances to control my life, which would result in my ending up dissatisfied. The dream was unequivocal, even though I didn't receive the "hard data" to support my misgivings until months later.

On the other hand, if you came to me and told me that you dreamed that you had found your autobiography and did not like the ending, and that, therefore, you were going to break up with your partner, I would have questions. For instance, is there hesitation or doubt in your relationship already? If not, if your relationship is healthy and nurturing, your version of this dream may mean that there is an area in your life—not necessarily in your romantic relationship—where you need to pay careful attention to a choice you have to make. Remember: Working with dreams can be as "universal as a heartbeat," but also as "individual as a fingerprint." Your dreams respond to the events in your own life—which will not be the same as events in mine. Your dreams will therefore use symbols that have meaning and clarity for you.

Another dream that had clear practical consequences was related to me by a colleague—a woman who was struggling in waking life with a decision of whether or not to buy a particular house. She was leaning toward the purchase because the price was very good, but she had doubts about the neighborhood and whether it would feel safe enough. Nor was she sure about the structural integrity of the house. During this stressful time, she dreamed that she walked into the house, which was nicely decorated, and discovered that a room at the back had a leaking ceiling. She decided the dream was telling her there might be something problematic in the house that was not immediately noticeable. The message from her unconscious was an alert that she pay attention to her fears regarding the home's quality. Rather than continuing to let it nag at her, she decided to have an inspection of the water and electrical systems in the house.

The point of these stories is not that the dreams were predictive, but that they each manifested concerns about major decisions that were pending. Basically, they presented options. My colleague was prompted to hire an inspector to correct or confirm her suspicions. Whether or not there were actual leaks in the house, the information would help her to make a more confident decision. For me, I learned that I needed to seize control of my life and decisions, to write my own ending. Of course, our dreams do not require that we take their advice. Instead, they give us options and opportunities for making choices in our waking lives.

Exercising free choice is so important—it is one of God's essential laws—but your unconscious offers input because it has a much broader perspective. The unconscious is always like today's newspaper, dealing with current events and giving you commentary, editorializing on those events. Editorials look to the past and describe current events in relation to it. Then they provide recommendations for current action. This is what dreams do as well. Dreams advise you and give you practical options for handling situations in your life. Whether or not you adopt those suggestions is up to you. Your free choice is always preserved. The difference is that, when you engage in free choice in accordance with and as an expression of the unconscious, you make choices informed by 95 percent of your awareness.

A beautiful instance of this came to me years ago in what was just a snippet of a dream. In the dream, I was shampooing my hair, which was long and black with streaks of grey in it. When I had the dream, my hair was still black; there was no grey in it. I considered what grey hair represented to me. The first word that came to mind was "wisdom." Considering that shampooing your hair means to clean it, and that your hair is what is on your head (closely associated with thoughts and ideas), I concluded that the message from my unconscious was a suggestion that I clean out some of my ideas—ideas that I had perhaps clung to beyond the point where they were useful. Had I dreamed of my hair being tangled and matted, I might have concluded that the message had to do with my ideas being confused—contorted and knotted. If I had dreamed of brushing my hair and it was flowing and shining, I might have taken it to mean that my ideas were harmonious and bright.

One way you can practice deciphering the practical messages you receive from the unconscious is by looking at commonplace dreams. For instance, many people have dreams of being back in school, or of appearing naked in public, or of losing their teeth. Let's look at the most common of these—the dream that you are back in school. Let's say you dream that you are in second grade. First, let's deconstruct that. What is a school? A school is a place where you are educated and socialized. What is second grade? The second grade is an early phase of schooling, a time when you learn basic, simple skills. Now think about what is going on in your life. Are your relationships at work or home feeling complicated? If so, perhaps this dream is saying that you need to go back to the basics, to repeat some of the basic learning you did at the very beginning of your experiences with other people—for example, saying "please" and "thank you" to show that you don't take a loved one for granted.

And what happens if you add the dimension of being naked? What is nudity? To be nude is to be without clothing, to have your body exposed. In our culture, this may represent feeling unprotected. Connecting this to the second grade, it may indicate that you are relearning basic principles, but feeling exposed and overwhelmed by the process. That is, if you dream that you are naked and also back in the second grade, you may be feeling so vulnerable and exposed by your feelings of inadequacy that you are denying your need to relearn basic principles. It really can be that simple.

And what if you dream that your teeth are falling out? This is an alarming dream, but remember that it is symbolic. Start slowly. What is the function of teeth? The most important function is to chew food for survival. But teeth also help us to speak, which is why people with no teeth often have difficulty enunciating. Thus teeth both help to bring food in and to let words out. So if you dream you are losing your teeth, it may indicate that you are losing your ability to take in whatever is going on in your life and also your ability to process and express it.

As you attempt to summarize messages from the unconscious, do your best not to exclude things, even if they seem insignificant. A friend of mine was recently recounting a dream that involved his fear of being judged negatively for developing his intuition—we'll look at this dream in more detail later. As he described the dream, he began rubbing his left knee. I noticed this, and asked him why he was doing it, because the body also speaks symbolically. Remember that the left side of the body is connected to feminine energy and the energy of all the women in your life. But your feminine energy is also your intuition, your creativity. By touching his left knee, my friend was expressing his restlessness and anxiety as it pertained to his intuition. Paying attention to subtle bodily responses as you work with your dreams may reveal the intent of your unconscious.

Responding to Dream Messages

When you are working to understand a dream's message, be careful not to modify its content through something like lucid dreaming—becoming aware that you are dreaming during a dream. Like many people, a friend with whom I have been doing dreamwork has become increasingly aware that she is dreaming during her dreams and that she can control and shape aspects of her dreams. But if you change the content or direction of a dream before you know what it is telling you, your unconscious will just knock at the door of your consciousness even more loudly and more insistently. For instance, if you alter a disturbing dream so that it has a pleasant ending, you may neutralize the dream's guidance and prompt your unconscious to present you with increasingly intense dreams, or even nightmares. If, on the other hand, you face the situation presented in the dream and deal with it in your waking life, your unconsious will respond by changing the dream or making it stop.

Here's a complex and fascinating example of how you can change a dream by changing your life. A friend had been experiencing a terrifying recurring dream since childhood. In it, she was back in her childhood home, feeling dread about approaching a scary space behind an attic partition in which she sensed a sinister presence. Although she is now over fifty, she had never looked behind that partition and still experiences a sense of horror about what exists in that space. Each time she had this particular dream, she woke from it with an urgent need to urinate. As a child, she had had frequent urinary tract infections (UTIs). Research has shown that, among children, there is a very high correlation between sexual abuse and recurring UTIs caused by bacteria that a child's system cannot handle and that causes irritation and infection. We concluded that her need to urinate following her recurring dream was a vestigial memory of the infections and abuse she had experienced as a child.

Overcoming these issues involved two steps. First, my friend needed to identify and understand her triggers—the situations in her daily, waking life that were making her feel the way she often felt while growing up. In other words, something in her adult life was replicating her childhood feelings of being unsafe or violated, feeling oppressed or molested. The intrusion in her adult life turned out to be not physical abuse, but invasive demands at work. And her body had learned to respond to this by signaling an urgent need to urinate.

After she identified her triggers, the second step was to retrain her body by changing her response to those triggers. To begin, we applied her dream to waking life and developed a method through which she could retrain her body to express anger or feelings of fear orally rather than through the urinary tract. She did this using a very simple exercise. She began taking two or three short breaks throughout the day, during which she paused at her desk and got up from her computer. Next, she took one deep breath and thought: Who am I really pissed at right now? My spouse? My boss? My mother? A friend or sibling? Sometimes the answer was as simple as the noise coming from construction across the street. The key was simply to note the source of her anger and give herself permission to express that feeling for no more than thirty seconds or a minute. Then she went to the lavatory and washed her hands with cold water, and sometimes splashed cold water on her face.

In order to stop the feeling of agitation, she let cold water fall on the insides of her wrists, where there are meridian and acupuncture points. Cold water hitting these points calms and soothes agitation. Some even claim that it can help with overcoming addiction. She completed the exercise by saying to herself: "I am expressing this now so that I do not need to express it at night." This gave her brain the message that she was not going to resist or suppress her feelings. Remember: Whatever we resist, persists. When you resist something, you create energy, and whatever you are resisting will keep pressing at you. Unless you confront it, it will just keep intruding on you, even though it has absolutely no power to do so on its own. The power is in your brain, your mind.

When you summarize a message from the unconscious, you can define the problem and begin to find a solution for it. This most often involves changing an approach that is not serving you. If you have a dysfunctional thought, acknowledge it and then take one long deep breath to transform your stress hormones into calming hormones. Confront whatever is troubling you and promise to revisit it later. Then keep that promise.

This technique operates on principles similar to those underlying most martial arts, which teach you to ground yourself, steady yourself where you are, and wait until you can turn the energy of an attack back on your opponent. Always wait for your opponent to get close, and never work from a distance. Then you can grab him, pull him in further, and flip him over. If you reach out too far to grab your opponent, you lose your balance. If you wait too long to defend yourself, your opponent may get too close and you will not have sufficient energy or power to counter the attack. When, however, you wait until you are just close enough, you can throw your opponent off balance and bring him down.

This same principle applies to dysfunctional thoughts. You cannot resist a troubling issue by holding it at a distance. You must acknowledge it and then wait until you are in a better position to confront it. When you do that, the message you send to your brain is that you are empowering yourself and taking control, rather than giving the thought energy by resisting it from a position of instability.

Eventually, my friend with the recurring dream about the horrible attic decided she had had enough, so she changed the way she dealt with her feelings of anger and invasion. She opened the door to the attic and approached the hidden space that had so terrified her since childhood. As soon as she pulled back the partition, she found a silly, little straw man—basically, a bale of straw with hands and legs. Rather than experiencing terror, she laughed because the figure was so absurd. Later, she told me that the "monster" reminded her of the straw man in the Wizard of Oz, a character who cried because he did not have a brain and felt so vulnerable and helpless. When she awoke from this iteration of the dream, she felt much better. In fact, even though the level of crisis in her life actually increased in the days to follow, she felt fortified and strengthened by her changed dream. By changing her dream, she changed herself and, by extension, her life.

Dream Characters and Settings

When considering dreams that explicitly involve your interactions with other people, you must remember that *the dreamer is always dreaming about the dreamer*. Other people in your dreams always represent various aspects of yourself or ways you feel that other people may perceive you. A friend of mine dreamed that she was naked and being taunted and mocked by a group of college students. The dream, which involved an audience, represented feeling exposed in front of others. Thus, in waking life, my friend was likely feeling self-conscious and embarrassed about something and did not trust her community or environment to support her. The students could have been aspects of herself—her own shame, for instance—or could simply have been stand-ins reflecting her experience in the waking world. The dream, however, was not really about the students who were mocking her; it was about my friend and how she felt.

When there are other characters in your dreams, they represent whatever is going on in your life—support, irritation, affection, anger. Another friend recently dreamed of her ex-partner. In fact, she was not actually dreaming about him, but rather what he represented in her life. When I asked her what her ex-partner symbolized, she answered: "Authority—admirable authority that is trustworthy, in charge, and also supportive." Later, however, she came to feel that this ex-partner was unreliable and unjust, which led to feelings of betrayal and, ultimately, to her decision to leave. To summarize the message from the unconscious, the ex-partner represented a beloved and supportive authority who became unreliable and undependable to the point where leaving was the only option.

Now, even five years later, if my friend has a stressful experience with her mother or her current boss—with anyone who holds authority in her life and may also have disappointed her—she dreams about her ex-partner. The dream's message is not about the ex-partner specifically, but about the position that person occupied and how that person's behavior affected her in the past. That is, the dream is saying that the experience she is having in the present is similar to the one she had in the past with her ex-partner. In the same way, whenever I dream that I am back in graduate school and have yet to finish my thesis—a traumatic time in my life—it alerts me right away that there is a situation in my waking life in which I feel I am being treated unfairly.

This multidimensionality is one of the great beauties of the unconscious. It can deliver multiple levels of representation through a single item or event. In its own kind of conservation of energy, it uses a few images, a few pictures, a few stories to efficiently convey its messages. When you examine the content of these messages, you understand that your dreams are not about a single person, time, or place, but rather about a variety of issues currently affecting your waking life. Each of the dream's players, settings, or objects is itself a summary of a more complex theme. Often, these items or characters will repeat themselves based on your attachments to them. In time, you will come to understand your own lexicon of symbols so that you can relate them to your life immediately, without having to go through the whole process of deconstruction.

One client, who was looking for a publisher for her first book, was unexpectedly—and hurtfully—dropped by her agent. That night, her ex-boyfriend appeared in a dream and leaned over to kiss her. She turned her face away and he ended up kissing the right side of her neck. Because we had worked closely with her dreams, she knew immediately upon awakening that this particular character represented the love of her life that she had lost. In a more general sense, he represented loss. The kiss indicated connection, or in this case, reconnection. The fact that she turned away showed her that she was not sure whether she wanted to accept this reconnection. Moreover, she understood that the right side of the body represents the left brain— the masculine energy, the part of her that is active, goal-oriented, and assertive. Because her agent had just dropped her, she felt dismayed and disheartened. In response, the dream sent her a personalized representation of loss to show that she had the option of reconnecting with what she had lost, even if she felt unsure about pursuing it. To summarize, the message from the unconscious was that she could be goal-oriented and assertive, and reconnect with lost opportunities in order to identify new ones.

Infants and children appear very commonly in dreams. Understanding why they occur and what they may indicate can help you as you begin to translate your dreams independently. Imagine, for example, that you dream you are walking on a sidewalk with a three-year-old boy. You are holding his hand when, all of a sudden, he lets go and runs into the street where he is struck by an oncoming truck. You wake up, terrified and shaking. What is the message from the unconscious?

Whenever your dreams feature a child, think about what was going on in your life when you were the age of the child in the dream—in this dream, when you were three years old. If you don't remember much about yourself at that age, don't overthink it. Just consider what your situation may have been at that age. Were you an eldest child who, around age three, was faced with the arrival of a new sibling? Were you a younger child treated dismissively by your older siblings? Did you lose someone at that age—a pet or even a family member? Reflect briefly on what that age and stage in your life may represent to you, even if you are not consciously aware of it in waking life. Alternatively, if you have children, what was uppermost in your life when your children were three years old? If your adult daughter experienced an intense illness at age three, you likely associate a child of that age with feelings of incredible anxiety and protectiveness.

If you are not able to associate any particular emotions or experiences from either yourself or your children at age three, you can also look at the dream more broadly. It seems fairly clear that this dream, on a very general level, also represents the way in which a childish, reactive stance can put you at great risk. Adults are proactive; children are reactive. Adults make choices and decisions and plans, and realize the consequences of their actions. An adult, for instance, will acknowledge that continually eating cheese sandwiches will result in feeling bloated and gaining weight. He or she can, therefore, decide to make a change, to take responsibility and stop eating those sandwiches. The childish reaction would be to think: "I feel kind of bad, but I just want to eat the cheese and I do not care about the consequences. If I feel bad later, it is probably just because the cheese was off or I have an ulcer."

For children, it is normal to avoid responsibility and ignore possible consequences. In this dream, the child simply reacts—I do not want to be under the control of an adult; I do not want to have my hand held—and thereby puts himself in a dangerous, threatening situation.

The cost of seizing his freedom without considering the wisdom of the adult hand (your adult mind, your higher self) is that he runs in front of a truck. The message from your unconscious may be that you are exposing yourself to danger (physical or emotional) by living your life in a way that is reactive, and not proactive.

This simple dream shows how, even in a dream involving a child, the dream is still about you. It is addressing the child in you. And, like all dreams, this one is also multidimensional. You do not have to be a parent to derive meaning from it. After all, a child being struck by a truck is a terrifying and horrifying event to anyone. You just have to follow the steps, interpret the symbols, and move forward.

Dreams and Healing

I strongly believe that the majority of disorders and imbalances in our lives are the result of issues like unaddressed emotional trauma, overstimulation, or lack of proper attention and nurturing at home. Our dreams are trying to show us that we have to look at all the traumas in our lives—all our wounding—because that is our truth. I do not mean that we are the sum of our injuries. Rather, we are the sum of all that we overcome. When we are able to look honestly at our wounds, we can find a way to heal them and strengthen ourselves. This allows us to make changes in our lives as adults, which, ultimately, allows us to love and appreciate ourselves and others.

Of course, along with facing our own wounds, we must also face the ways in which we may have wounded others. Guilt has existed since time immemorial, but, like fear or injury, guilt is counterproductive to growth. It should be acknowledged, faced, and then left behind. Wallowing in guilt does not strengthen us morally or spiritually, but instead keeps us feeling like victims. Whether we are consciously aware of it or not, however, we choose our lives and paths based on what we most need to learn, and both the conscious mind and the unconscious are expressions of the soul's journey. We repeat the stories of our lives not because we are foolish, but because we are trying to heal past trauma. This is why you have likely replicated patterns in your relationships, whether working, romantic, or social. You reexperience these patterns because each repetition provides a new opportunity to change your behavior and approach things differently. Once you alter your unconstructive patterns, you advance your healing and learning—advance, not complete, because, as long as you are alive, you are developing.

Still, we set up so many barriers to distract ourselves from facing our most vital truths. One of the most common ways we do this is by minimizing our fears and wounds by comparing them to what other people have experienced. But comparing your story to the stories of others does not help you maintain perspective; it only helps you to evade your own truth. Comparing yourself to others keeps you from being honest and truthful with yourself, and being honest and truthful with yourself is the only way to heal. Put simply, you rob yourself of your truth in the present when you whitewash your history.

Thus, when a friend of mine who is struggling with her self-esteem dismissively states that her childhood "was not that bad, relatively speaking" simply because she was never beaten or sexually abused, she believes she is being realistic, when what she is really doing is avoiding the truth. I challenged her when she said this, giving her permission to acknowledge her wounds, no matter how small she believed them to be in the grand scheme of the universe. As she became more forthcoming, she was able to admit that she had never learned to care for herself emotionally because she did not feel special to her mother. This was a true revelation for her. You see, by simply skipping the whitewash of her personal history, she was able to identify the source of her current issues and to consider ways to move beyond them. Ignoring your history is how you suppress your past; acknowledging it is how you begin to change your present, your current waking life.

As you work through step 6, remember that the unconscious is you, speaking to yourself. It is not another person or agent directing you. Rather, it is your higher self, the Divine in you, illuminating areas in your life that may be murky. Once you have defined and identified a dream's message and how it relates to your waking life, you can begin to adjust your attitudes or behaviors and feel better. As you continue to discover the meanings behind the symbols in your dreams, you will find yourself able to relate them to your waking life more and more quickly.

* * * * * * * * * * * * * * * * * *

To sum up...

1. Reflect on the work you have done in steps 1 through 5.

2. Try to summarize your dream's content in one or two clear messages from the unconscious.

3. Remember that the message is not literal, but symbolic.

4. Keep your interpretation simple, grounded in common sense, and relevant to your current, waking life.

5. Honor your work. Though it may initially be challenging, step 6 prepares you to understand the dream's guidance.

CHAPTER 11

Step 7. Consider Your Dream's Guidance for Waking Life

L ike newspapers, dreams report on current events and provide commentary and guidance. Whether or not you follow the advice is up to you. As I have explained, we always have free choice. But when we engage in free choice informed by both our conscious mind and our unconscious, we make better, more confident choices.

Determining what your dream is guiding you to do, like anything, becomes easier with practice and repetition. With practice, you will find that you are able to make sense out of the information your dreams provide and to make positive changes in your life based on that information more quickly and more successfully. What follows are examples of the kinds of advice dreams can provide, and what happens when you follow that advice.

Dream Stories

Messages from the unconscious are conveyed as stories—as drama. For instance, at a time when I had made some huge changes in my life, I began to dream that I was going outside to run. Although I had never exercised regularly, my unconscious was telling me that I needed to get moving—literally. In waking life, I felt trapped by some unhealthy patterns in my lifestyle and by my body's resistance to exercise. In the dream, however, I could run easily. Put simply, the dream was pointing out that I was capable of running, and it was advising me to get started.

So finally, I decided to take that advice. I started running. Over several months, I gradually worked up to running up to a mile comfortably, but in short spurts. Eventually, I learned a new way to breathe while running that allowed me to run a mile continuously. It was like an epiphany. Soon, I was able to run continuously for far longer distances and far more comfortably than I had during those first few runs. This not only restored my confidence in my body, it affirmed that, with baby steps and persistence, I could build skills of which I had never believed myself capable. When we address our dreams rather than ignoring or changing them, and simply change our behavior in waking life, we not only stop stressful dreams, we also become healthier and more confident.

Take, for instance, the guidance that recently came to a dear friend who has been living with cancer. He has been frustrated with the lack of progress in his treatment and with the toxicity and side effects of that treatment. A few months ago, he dreamed that his doctor advised him to look into a new, promising cancer treatment that had fewer side effects and was also more effective than his current program. In the dream, his doctor provided him with the long, chemical name of the treatment regimen. When he said he would not be able to remember the words, the doctor told him to just remember three letters. When he awoke the next morning, he looked up the letters and learned that the emerging treatment was real. Oddly, however, neither he nor his physician had heard of it before.

Though it may not seem so at first, this is an absolutely stunning example of the fact that your dreams are always about you. It was not my friend's doctor who revealed the treatment to him; it was his own unconscious posing as a representation of a caregiver, urging him to find a new treatment that would be better for his body, and would improve his prognosis and his life in general. Although the treatment was unknown to his conscious mind, his unconscious guided him not to accept the current, ineffective therapies that were making him so ill, but rather to seek better alternatives.

Sexual dreams quite often offer very clear and easily interpreted guidance. These dreams are very common, so it is useful to consider what they may offer as advice for your waking life. One dream that nearly all of us have experienced is that we are having sex with an old flame. Imagine that you dream you are having sex with a former lover whom you have not seen in twenty years. You may wake up and wonder why you dreamed about having sex with someone from your past that you never think about anymore. But the dream most likely has nothing to do with having sex literally; sex is merely the drama, the story, of the dream.

To apply such a dream to your waking life, start at the beginning. What is having sex? What does it mean? Sex is literally one body in some way entering another; it is a symbolic expression of the deepest level of intimacy or closeness that one person can have with another. In terms of the unconscious, sex is thus often less concerned with the physical act and more representative of one person experiencing intimacy with another.

In dreams, you can experience intimacy with men, women, or friends because the sex most likely has nothing to do with either sexual orientation or sexual desire. Rather, it has to do with emotional closeness in some aspect of your life. If you have a dream about a former lover, consider what qualities that person represents, what he or she represents in your life. For instance, a friend described a dream in which she was having sex with the first boyfriend she had as a teenager. When I asked her to tell me the first word that came into her mind regarding what he represented to her now, she immediately said: "Joy."

To analyze the dream, we first identified what was uppermost in her life. She reported feeling overworked and stressed out in her relationship with her current boyfriend. Thus, her unconscious was alerting her to those dormant feelings of anxiety and dissatisfaction, and advising her to try bringing the feeling of joy into her intimate relationships. My friend was surprised to hear this; in fact, she was actually very surprised that she had described the old boyfriend as representing joy in the first place! Why this word, then? Because her unconscious wanted her to hear it, wanted to urge her to get close to some joy. In fact, her dream had nothing to do with having sex with the old boyfriend. Instead, it was a lovely reminder that she needed to let go of some of the stress in her life and to experience joy again, intimately—to feel what she felt when she looked back on that relationship from long ago.

Of course, when you dream about sex, it may have something to do with sex in general on one level, because sex simply provides the context. At a slightly deeper level, however, it may have to do with sex in your current, waking life. For instance, had my friend described feeling joy with her current partner, the dream would have seemed less a reminder to seek out joy and more a celebration of the joy she was experiencing. However, because she was not experiencing joy or pleasure in her present-day relationship, her dream made a suggestion. The suggestion was in no way an indication that she unconsciously wanted to reunite with her old boyfriend, but rather that she needed to find a way to experience joy in her current waking life and, perhaps, with her current boyfriend.

It is important to keep in mind that dream stories like this are not about nostalgia and should not be dismissed as such. Dreaming of your youth does not mean that you long to return to the time when you were young and did not have any problems. Let's face it; you did have problems back then—different problems, perhaps. These problems may not seem as urgent to you now, but they were probably very real and overwhelming at the time. The idea that dreams merely represent wishful thinking—in this case, the assumption that my friend's dream revealed a desire to reunite with her old boyfriend—is erroneous and misses the point just as much as Jung's notion of the collective unconscious does.

We need to bring our dreams back down to earth—to bring their stories to bear on our current waking lives. The interpretation of your dreams need not be useful to all humankind; it just has to be useful to you. After all, you and your life story are this book's true subjects, and also the subject of all of your dreams. Your dreams, your unconscious, and the wisdom they provide are all about you. You alone are the repository of your own soul, your own life, your own story. You are therefore an important expression of divine energy.

It is all too easy to regard your dreams as simply expressions of longing for a time when you did not have any "real" worries, a time when life was somehow different, better, simpler. Frankly, you do yourself a disservice when you take that route. If my friend had dismissed her dream as mere nostalgia, she might have ended up spending the following day feeling sorry for herself and longing for the past, rather than realizing that she needed and could have the experience of joy in her life right now. When you consider the images in your dreams on a symbolic, not a literal, level, you can profit from their guidance. And do not overthink the message, or you may lose it.

In fact, there are many parallels between dream interpretation and artistic creation. In creating art—whether literary, musical, or graphic —a person shares his or her symbols with an external audience. When you dream, your unconscious shares your symbols with you. If you have ever taken an art class or taken up a new creative pursuit, you were probably told what I have been telling you here: Perfectionism is limitation. In artistic creation, you must be careful not to overthink what you are expressing and how you are expressing it, because logic can limit your imagination. Do not allow the editor or critic inside you to restrain your creative wisdom. There will be time for refinement later. The way to make progress now is to dive in with as little self-consciousness as possible.

In the same way, when you are seeking the guidance in your dreams, be careful not to overthink or worry about "getting it right." There is no one right answer, which is kind of the point. So if your ex-lover inspires you to describe him or her with the word "joy," just say it! Do not talk yourself out of it; just go with your first instinctive reaction. With practice, determining the messages contained within your dreams will grow increasingly simple and evident.

As we go through life, our stories change. But these changes occur a lot more slowly and with greater difficulty if you ignore 95 percent of your potential wisdom. Working with your dreams allows you to move much more swiftly through difficult changes in your life. If you work consistently with the unconscious, if you become more aware of your dreams and pay attention to their messages, if you become more aware of your history—of your own story—you can make changes that are more relevant today. You can be proactive and not reactive. And the more dreams you work with, the more wisdom you will access. I first started recording my dreams in the early 1980s. When I look through my dream records as I prepare to give a presentation, lecture, or workshop, it is utterly fascinating to me how dreams from decades ago apply just as easily to my life today as they did to my life back then. Moreover, these records remind me of the amazing ways in which I have changed and grown over the last three decades.

Bathroom Dreams

Many people have "bathroom dreams," dreams involving feces or urine that represent the body's shedding of toxins and waste. This may be your unconscious saying that you are or you need to be cleansing yourself, or that there is a toxic dynamic between you and someone or something in your life.

When I began recording my dreams, I did not understand the richness of the unconscious at all. Although I was interested in dreams, I certainly did not understand their true value. I only began to record them when I joined a dream-study group. As I catalogued my dreams, I opened myself up to a whole new world. At the time, although I was already a practicing clinical psychologist, I had never had any formal training in dream interpretation. As a result, I simply went along with everything that the study-group leader said. Although her interpretations often veered toward the negative, the process was very interesting and fascinating to me. Eventually, however, some discord emerged between the group leader and the group members. The group was clearly disintegrating and I was very perturbed. After the group dissolved, however, my interest in dreams continued.

I remember having an extremely upsetting dream not long thereafter and wondering what I was going to do without an interpreter to help me analyze it. In the dream, I was in a public bathroom and began to have a bowel movement. The commode began to overflow with waste until it was everywhere, all over everything. I was devastated and humiliated, and the smell was so noxious and potent that it actually woke me up. When I awoke, however, there was no smell.

But the intensity of the smell in the dream was part of the message my unconscious was sending to my conscious mind.

When I told a friend about the dream, she simply asked me how I would interpret it if I were working with a patient. I answered that there was BS going on in my waking life that I obviously needed to address, because the odor was so strong. When I thought about it, it became very clear to me that there was a lot of conflict going on in an area of my life that had become very important to me—my interest in dream interpretation and the dissolution of my study group. My dream was clear guidance to pay attention to my feelings about a destructive situation affecting my waking life. I will always be grateful to my friend for not attempting to interpret that dream for me, but rather showing me that I was capable of doing it for myself. This is how I learned in a very simple and gentle way that I was capable of doing my own dreamwork.

This dream was especially dramatic because I woke up smelling a noxious odor, which was my unconscious telling me to pay attention. Essentially, the dream was a nightmare. But its intensity derived from my urgent need to separate from the group leader because there were so many negative dynamics emerging within the group that participation was becoming genuinely harmful, threatening. My dream served as a wake-up call to disconnect and move on immediately. With the confidence I derived from this message, I was able to move on without anger. Having recognized that the group dynamic was not healthy for me personally, I simply told the group leader that I was leaving and wished her the best. After all, she had inspired me to begin thinking about dreams, so I was grateful.

This dream shows why following the guidance given you in your dreams is so important. If you neglect your dreams and they are attempting to convey something of grave importance, they will get more and more intense, until they become nightmares. As scary as these dreams can be, however, they are intended as support and guidance. Just remember that your unconscious will knock as loudly as it has to until you answer the door.

I followed the steps that I share with you here to discover the message of my bathroom dream and determine its guidance. I slowly repeated the dream aloud, then I considered what a bowel movement and an overflowing public toilet could represent. At its most basic, the first represented getting rid of waste, waste pouring out, while the latter represented the fear that everyone would see and notice the toxic matter. Taken literally, the intense smell indicated that I was ill or had consumed something harmful to me—something that was really wreaking havoc with my system.

Thus, the dream was showing me that, whatever this noxious material was, it was a result of consuming—taking in—something very bad, very toxic. What was uppermost in my life at that time was my relationship with the group leader, which had become so problematic that her actions were exposing me to physical, emotional, and, potentially, legal risk. The dream was a message from my unconscious that I wanted and needed to go my own way. Once I observed and understood the message, I was able to take action. Had my dream not brought my fears and needs to my attention so forcefully, it might have taken me more time to act upon them, which would have meant exposing myself to more hurt and risk.

Control Dreams

If there is a stressful situation in your waking life and you choose to do nothing about the problem when it is presented to you in a dream, the dream will keep coming back. It may not be a recurring dream *per se*; it may take different forms. One night, you may dream that a new boss is forcing you to do your job the wrong way; another night, you may dream you are a passenger in a car driven by someone who is making decisions that put you at risk. In either case, the message is the same. You need to take control of your life and not hand your decisions and feelings over to someone else.

Dreams may take many different forms and yet deliver the same message. In fact, you may even have a series of interrelated dreams. If you ignore them, your unconscious will ultimately give you the dream as a nightmare. You may dream again of being a passenger in someone else's car. But this time, the driver may refuse to slow down until the car careens off a bridge. Now you are falling, panicked and totally overwhelmed. Just as in its earlier, gentler version, this dream is guiding you to take control of your life. But now it is also showing you that not taking control may lead to very serious and harmful consequences.

People who dream of scenarios like this often wake up thinking the dreams are predictive—that they will soon be in an accident. This is not necessarily true. On one level, the dream may actually be telling you that it is time to check the brakes on your car, to confirm your vehicle's reliability and stability. On another level, however, it may be telling you that if you had been driving—if you had been in control— an emotionally damaging situation in your waking life may be or may have been avoided. It is the same message, just delivered more dramatically. If you ignore that advice, it will get louder, shaking you to wake you up and compelling you to action. When someone knocks at your door and you answer, they stop knocking. It is the same when you act on the guidance your unconscious provides you. When you act, there is no need for the dream, theme, or nightmare to return. There is no need to confront you with your anxieties, because you are now doing something about them.

A client who was a talented dancer—we'll call her Barbara—had a blood disease that put her at high risk for stroke. To treat the illness, she was taking various very strong medications that had many side effects. I asked her how long she had to continue this therapy, and she replied sadly: "For a long, long time." Barbara had a dream in which she was traveling on a train that kept going in and out of tunnels. The train car alternated between brilliant sunlight and dark shadow as it moved through the dream landscape. In the car were two women—one beautiful and white-haired, the other plain. The beautiful woman wore an elegant white robe and a pendant that hung between her breasts. The stone in the pendant looked white, but reflected all the colors of the spectrum. The other, more humble-looking woman wore only a simple white robe. My client awoke with a strong feeling of encouragement, a belief that she would heal from her illness.

What was this dream advising her to do? Let's begin with the train. A train is a vehicle that takes you from point A to point B. Unlike a car, however, it is constrained by a track, an established path. For Barbara, the beautiful woman with white hair evoked a spiritual guide—an angel or manifestation of Mother Nature. But she also represented wisdom and the ability to heal. The tunnels represented birth canals, passages on the other side of which is an opening. Reemergence. Rebirth. This dream, which was so brief, was, in fact, very rich. Although it didn't contain a lot of action, it was very clear and encouraging.

Barbara realized that the humble woman reflected her humility in the face of her illness, whereas the wise woman represented her strength, her ability to heal. It was this aspect of herself that was wearing the beautiful pendant, which lay directly over her heart chakra and reflected a healing light that radiated from her own heart and wisdom. She may thus be going through a process of death (medications), only to be reborn (healed). Barbara's dream is guiding her to persevere—to stay in control—even though her treatment may be unpleasant. It is also reminding her that, although she may feel humbled by her illness, her true strength radiates from her own heart, her own wisdom.

Another friend has a particularly interesting recurring dream that takes place in her home—a bungalow with a basement, a main floor, and an attic. In the dream, she is aware that a demon resides within the house—on the main floor most of the time, although sometimes he lurks in the attic or in the basement behind the furnace. He is always confined to one small area, but she knows that he wants to come out to scare her. In her dreams, she argues with him and orders him to stay hidden and not to come out. To uncover the guidance within the dream, we took it through the steps.

After repeating the dream slowly, my friend titled it "The Demon in the House." She struggled to identify what was most on her mind in waking life, so we skipped ahead, defining the dream's objects to our Martian. She described a house as a nice, enclosed shelter where people live and feel safe, with running water, plumbing, and lights. At first, she had difficulty defining the demon, because she never actually sees him in the dream. She does, however, feel his presence as a negative force, an evil spirit. So I asked her to describe evil, which she defined as the bad side of people, something that brings pain and destruction, leaving people feeling hurt, scared, unsafe, injured in body and mind. To understand the guidance in this dream, then, we needed to explore what the unconscious was trying to convey by presenting a dark, injurious force in my friend's home—the place where she lives and should feel safe.

I asked her where in her waking life she experienced feelings like those the demon evoked, noting that the situation may be one she was not seeing (which is why, in the dream, she can never see the demon). Where did she feel hurt, scared, unsafe? And why did the demon appear in her home—not at her bank or at her office? At first, she thought that perhaps she was oppressing herself. Indeed, one of the dangers of assuming that your dreams are always about you is the risk of not examining the influence of external people or situations in your waking life. As we talked, she realized that she had been feeling that she was not getting praise or support from her partner or family for her accomplishments, even though her accomplishments were remarkable—she had survived multiple life-threatening injuries and completed an advanced degree late in life.

By considering the behavior of these other people in the context of her dream, Barbara was able to look at her life with more clarity and identify changes she could make to improve the situation. She decided to begin praising herself. By doing so, she manifests the belief that she is capable and remarkable, so that others will begin to believe it and appreciate it in her. "The Demon in the House" is a frightening dream, but its intent is positive. It prompts her to look at what is really going on in her personal life. It shows her that, deep down, she does not feel safe, that she feels oppressed and hurt, and therefore can not move forward. She needs to take control and make changes.

By believing in herself and demanding in a firm and nonaccusatory way that her loved ones not put her down, my friend will reinforce her confidence and put an end to her persistent anxiety. Once she has done this, her dream will inevitably change. The next time the demon makes his presence known, she will not be afraid to face him. She will acknowledge him and even appreciate him for what he is—a symbol intended to clarify her life. But this will only happen is she takes control and does the work in her waking life.

Nightmares and negative dreams become more persistent and disturbing when we do not pay attention to the quieter messages from our unconscious. When you pay attention to your dreams and make corresponding changes in your life, you begin to have fewer and fewer nightmares. Understand, however, that your nightmares will never stop entirely. And, believe it or not, this is a good thing. As long as you live, you will have work to do. Even if you attend to every dream you recall, there will still be room for the occasional nightmare, simply because you are not trained or encouraged to recall your dreams and thus do not remember the majority of them. Nightmares, however, you remember. That is why your unconscious occasionally sends them to you, trying to get your attention with a bigger, louder voice. And sometimes it has to scream.

From Darkness into Light

Step 7 of my process of dream analysis is perhaps the most illuminating, because the core purpose of a dream is always to encourage you to look at yourself and deal with your fears and issues on your own, so that you can move toward the light beyond the darkness. That is really the single most important message of any dream. No matter how dark life gets, there is always light beyond. In dreams and in waking life, you should therefore never walk in fear. Focus on the blessings in your life— on what is already available to you—and those blessings will increase. If you find yourself longing for more money, try replacing the word "money" with the word "blessings." Long for more blessings to come into your life instead, and they will. And perhaps in surprising ways.

An old Chinese proverb tells of a farmer's son who falls from his horse. He breaks his leg in the fall and can no longer help with the farming. The villagers come by to visit, saying: "How horrible! It is terrible that your son broke his leg and cannot help with the farm." The farmer trusts in the Divine, however, and refuses to judge events as good or bad. He simply responds: "We will see." Soon, a war breaks out and all the young men in the village are drafted to fight, but the farmer's son is spared because of his broken leg. Now the villagers come to him and say: "Oh, you are so lucky that your son broke his leg, because it kept him from the war." Again, he simply says: "We will see."

This is what I mean when I say that blessings sometimes arrive in unexpected ways. In our culture, we so often jump to darkness, to despair. For instance, if you lose your job, it may seem unfortunate, but it may also be an opportunity to open another door. If you trust that things will work out, you will find a way forward. But sometimes, we talk ourselves out of opportunities before we even try. The opportunities are there, but we need to do our part to keep moving forward. In fact, one of the simplest ways to define the purpose of our lives is this: Keep on moving.

When you do nothing, you start to feel terrible. When you put your energy, your focus, and your beliefs into the negative and scarier aspects of situations and events, they get worse. On the other hand, when you face those fears, you develop tools to transcend them. This is why popular self-help methods are not useful. If you only consider the positive, you deprive yourself of the opportunity to consider the darker side of life. By looking directly at the reality of the darkness and surviving it, however, you strengthen yourself and your faith. You may have all the faith in the world, but if you do not put the work in or if you allow your fear or foolishness or impassivity to control you, you will miss out on all the available blessings and opportunities. All actions have consequences. We understand that we are precious children of the Divine, but God intended us to be co-creators. With each choice, each second, each breath, we can create any kind of life we want.

Years ago, I dreamed that I was sitting in a plain room across from a man who was giving me a psychological test. His son was seated on his left, his wife on his right. I fell asleep right in front of him while being tested and felt devastated. I titled the dream "Being Irresponsible." What was going on in my life at that time? I had a general feeling that I was not attending properly to the tests of my soul or my life; I felt checked out. I was also experiencing tremendous anxiety because my practice as a therapist was faltering, both because I felt it was time for me to move on to other passions and interests, and because I was focused on writing my first book. With fewer patients, I was unsure how to manage my income. I was tempted to earn money by doing psychological testing, but did not find that nearly as satisfying as therapy.

My fear and anxiety were driving my decision-making; I was fearful that I would make a decision that would make me feel worse in my life. In the dream, I am taking a psychological test, but I am asleep— not present. I am being irresponsible. But the dream also showed that I was willing to take the risk of not doing the testing—sleeping through it. This helped me to clarify how I was feeling and to make a decision based not on fear, but on what I wanted in my life.

Around the same time, I dreamed that I was younger, thinner, pregnant, and moving into a new home. I was preparing for the birth. My hair was dark and I was making the move on my own, with no assistance. I felt positive and eager about both moving and preparing for the baby. At the time of the dream, I was sixty-two, so the dream was not indicating that I might, in fact, be pregnant. Rather, pregnancy is a time of preparation and development; babies are literally new beginnings. The younger body and new home symbolized movement toward a new way of being—healthier, younger in spirit. And I felt good about doing this all on my own. If I had considered the dream to be merely predictive, I might have dismissively assumed that it meant I would someday be thin and dark-haired and positive about my prospects. But I did not consider the dream predictive; it showed me a possibility of how things could be if I did the work, and if I took accountability for doing that work on my own. So I changed my diet; I began exercising and caring for my body. Sure enough, I have become healthier, thinner, and more positive about my prospects.

A close friend with whom I work frequently dreamed that she, her mother, a child, and I were sitting in a kitchen admiring souvenirs she had purchased on vacation—swords and knives that were finely honed. She kept telling the child to be careful because the swords were very sharp, and she demonstrated this by slicing a piece of paper. What are swords? They are sharp and dangerous, but also can be wielded with skill. Now, weapons can represent violence, anger. But in my friend's dream, she is showing off the weapons, not feeling angry at all. This simply shows that she is proud of and managing her emotions. By collecting them, she can learn to use them.

Then my friend revealed an element in the dream that she had been embarrassed to share at first. The swords had feces on their edges. She was trying to hide an unpleasant part of the expression of her anger and her competence managing it. When we discussed this, she admitted that she was afraid of her own power. Throughout her life, she had made strong wishes for certain circumstances to occur in her life, and each time something frightening had happened that enabled those circumstances to occur. I pointed out that this did not have to be a source of fear. The frightening things had occurred in her childhood and adolescence. Would you give a sword to a child or adolescent? Of course not. But an adult can handle one responsibly and, with practice, skillfully. Thus, in the dream, she is proud of her powers and managing them. She is also showing the child within her that power can be beautiful if managed, but can also be dangerous. It's all about balance.

Fear and Guilt

What you see and believe and experience in your unconscious manifests in your body. Guiding yourself through imagery from your unconscious—whether received in a dream or a trance state—can thus be useful when you must face something difficult, something that is having a negative effect on your life. I advised my friend to reconsider her dream of the swords—and the fear of her own power that the dream represented—by reentering the dream with the intent to heal. By retrieving the swords and cleansing the tips—swabbing them and disinfecting them until they were sharp and clean—she could acknowledge her power without a sense of shame or embarrassment. She could then repeat the interaction with the child, letting the child see her use the clean swords safely and skillfully.

When my friend disowned her power, she disowned an aspect of herself that her soul had striven for in the past. By staying in shame, she undermined her own progress. But when you face the aspects of yourself that disturb and frighten you, when you see that you can manage them, you can move beyond shame. When you feel fear, you restrict your options. If you're terrified of germs, for example, you may restrict your physical contact with others. If you're terrified of flying in a plane, you may restrict your travels.

A friend who quit smoking a decade ago has a recurring dream in which she starts smoking again. She began her analysis of the dream by giving it the title "Caught Smoking Again." When I asked her how she felt when she awoke from the dream, she said she felt guilty, as if she had really smoked a cigarette. It made her feel like a bad person. She came to realize, however, that she was not feeling ashamed about smoking specifically, but rather about having broken a rule.

Guilt can be an important factor in dreams and it creates a very particular dynamic. My friend noted that, when the dream began, she felt her action was just plain wrong; but, as the dream continued, she felt less so. Because the dream recurs, however, there has to be something more to it than simply enjoying a dream cigarette! I asked her to think about her daily life, the things that were most on her mind of late, and then to think about what the dream may be trying to tell her. She answered that she felt a pull to break the rules—all the stipulations and regulations she was expected to obey at work and in society. In her life, she felt she had to go along with what everyone else wanted; but in her dreams, she could do whatever she wanted. She could smoke.

Feeling this way is understandable, but the dream has more to offer. I asked her what she did with this information, how she managed this sense of entitlement. She answered that, not wanting to buy the cigarettes, she borrowed them from her sister. She and her sister had smoked together when they were teenagers, although they had what she described as a "miserable" relationship at that time. Her current relationship with her sister, however, is good. So she is returning to a past experience of conflict, of breaking the rules, because it is related to something going on in her present. I asked her what was going on in her life right now with someone who is like a sister, in the sense of always being around. She revealed that the level of conflict in her relationship with her partner was very high. Her unconscious, then, was indicating to her that she needed to address her feelings about her partner.

In the dream, my friend breaks the rules and does whatever she wants; she gives herself permission to smoke. But the dream would not recur if it had gotten her attention and she had responded by making changes in her daily life. So I asked her what made her most unhappy at present in her waking life, and she returned to her feeling of being constrained by rules at every turn in her life. So, instead of acting out rule-breaking in her unconscious, she needs to begin connecting that behavior to her waking life so that her body and mind will be healthier. The dream was not advising her to go out and start breaking every rule. It was guiding her to make conscious choices as an adult. After all, if she simply rejects every rule, she is assuming the reactive stance of a child.

Eventually, my friend decided that what she really needed to do was just lighten up. She had been living by an internalized set of rules and judging herself harshly for breaking them. For instance, she believed that she personally had to fix everything that ever broke in her home.

When faced with having to call a professional to make the repairs that she could not, she at first felt like a failure. Then she told herself to take a breath, that there was no rule forbidding her to seek help and that she was going to be okay. If she had simply gone back to sleep to dream about smoking, it would not have helped her in her conscious life at all, and the dream would have kept tugging at her to pay attention.

Instead, by making a conscious decision to look at the dream and connect the dots leading back to her waking life, she identified a profound and basic truth—that she did not have to circumscribe her life with a set of arbitrary rules that she then felt guilty for breaking. When she acknowledged that she was responding judgmentally to breaking her own perceived rules, she could lighten up. The dream showed her that she wanted to break the rules, to do what she wanted. But if she had stopped there, she would not have been able to figure out the more significant message—that letting her world be controlled by rules, either external or self-imposed, was having a negative impact on her life right now. That is the value of dreams.

Incidentally, this is another example of how changing a dream before you have fully received its message can interfere with the communication from your unconscious. If you do not realize why you are dreaming something, you cannot learn from it. Until you let the dream deliver its message and then act on it, you are not communicating with your unconscious effectively. If you keep dreaming of drowning, ask yourself why. You are likely overwhelmed and feel you cannot breathe, that you are suffocating. Once you have received that message, you can start looking at the present—only the present, not the past, not even the unconscious. Then you can act upon the message. Once you have done this, you can change the dream to whatever you like.

Applying Dream Lessons

Because there is no time in the unconscious, we can apply dreams from the past to the present and they will still have relevance. Recently, as I read through some of my recorded dreams, I was struck by one from several years ago when I was faced with the daunting task of publicizing my first book. I dreamed that my mother had cancer in her legs. In the dream, she and I and the rest of my family were utterly horrified. I decided to care for her by feeding her only fresh fruits and vegetables.

As I considered the dream, I ran it through the process. Legs get you from point A to point B. I adored my mother, but she was very passive, and passive people often become passive-aggressive. My mother, who was an excellent cook and beloved by all, was unable to walk comfortably. Since the dreamer is always dreaming about the dreamer, my mother, of course, represented me in my own life. So the message of the dream was that, in order for me to move forward in my life and work, I could not be passive. I had to take care of myself and take charge. Unfortunately, I did not fully heed the message of this dream. Looking back, I realize that, if I had—if I had been proactive in publicizing my first book—my message would have reached even more people. This is precisely why this dream, from all the dreams I have recorded in the past, stood out to me. It carried advice that I had not yet fully perceived or accepted.

When you apply the message of your dreams—even dreams from the past—to your everyday life, you can make great progress. Ask yourself what you are seeing or how you are seeing things today, or maybe how you felt and viewed the world yesterday. Do not judge or edit, just observe and embrace. Even if you only spend a few minutes on your dreams each day, you will move forward; the effect is cumulative. To enhance the substance of each small step forward, acknowledge each one as you take it. For instance, if your dreams have helped you realize that you are reserved with your affection, try to note when you are feeling or have felt emotionally withdrawn during the day. When you note it, make a choice to be affectionate. Then act on it. Just as you encourage your own child as he or she begins to walk, be gentle and encouraging with yourself. Persistence—just a little bit of work every day—is all it takes to make a change. Honoring the steps you make toward change infuses them with conscious awareness.

* * * * * * * * * * * * * * * * *

To sum up...

1. Repeat aloud the message you summarized in step 6.

2. Consider the symbolic solutions offered in the dream.

3. Translate the symbolic advice into commonsense guidance related to current situations in your waking life.

4. If the dream does not seem to offer solutions, consider what steps you can take to address the issues raised in the dream.

5. Consider one or two tangible actions you can take in response to the dream's guidance.

6. Honor your baby steps.

Part III

Working
with Dreams

CHAPTER 12

Working with Simple Dreams

B y now, I trust I've made the value of repetition and practice perfectly clear. This section provides examples based on real conversations I've had with clients and friends while exploring real dreams. Observing the seven steps as they unfold illustrates what the actual process is like, which will help you get a feel for each individual step. I hope that reading through these dialogs—and, hopefully, beginning some of your own—will deepen your understanding of how the steps work, and why following them is so valuable.

This first example shows how you can gather a lot of information from an extremely brief dream. Because images are worth a thousand words, the message in a dream is often compressed. Going through the seven steps can help you find the surprisingly rich messages in even the simplest dreams.

In this dream, "D" dreamed about a bra—just a bra. When she wondered why she would think about a bra, I advised her to stop thinking about it and just note it. Then we began to go through the steps.

DEC: What is a bra for?

D: To support your breasts.

DEC: Now describe a bra and breasts to our Martian friend. Imagine that you are describing something that should be obvious to most people. But don't assume it is obvious in any way. Your unconscious talks in an extremely concentrated fashion. And remember that a picture is worth a thousand words.

D: Breasts are mounds of fat on a woman's chest that also feed babies. A bra holds them in place so they don't sag and bounce around.

DEC: So, breasts are very important because they feed babies. What are babies?

D: They are parasites that grow up and suck the life out of you.

DEC: Parasites? Things you want to get rid of and destroy?

D: No, you nurture them until they grow up.

DEC: You nurture a parasite?

D: Yes, you have to take care of it and nurture it, feed it, and change it.

DEC: Why?

D: So that it grows up to be its own individual.

DEC: Why do you want it to grow up to be its own individual?

D: Because we want to maintain the species.

DEC: Yes, survival. So you feed a baby because it is very helpless and will not survive on its own. Now let's get back to your bra. A bra supports this very important part of the body that is essential for the survival of the species.

D: Wow—that was a lot to come from just one word.

In this dream, the simple image of a bra, when we had to think about it in the simplest way possible, led us to the message of the dream. I am a woman and I wear a bra to support my breasts, which feed little babies, which ensures the survival of the species. When you do this, the intention of the dream becomes very clear.

* * * * * * * * * * * * * * * * *

To sum up...

1. You can gather a lot of information from an extremely brief dream.

2. Dream messages are often compressed into very dense images.

3. By deconstructing the dense images in even simple dreams, you can make their message clear.

CHAPTER 13

Inventing Dreams

As we've discussed, dreams are like the unconscious's version of today's newspaper: *The Daily Dreamer*. Your dreams, like a newspaper, report current events—today's events—but they also provide equally important editorials—commentary about those events. Your dreams will always deal with whatever is uppermost in your life right now. Recently, to help a friend understand how this works, I guided her through a useful exercise in which we made up a dream. This can be enormously helpful to beginners, who have yet to remember much of their dreams. It can also be useful for advanced dreamers who want to access the unconscious during waking hours. The two most important things to remember when attempting this are:

* Always consider what is uppermost in your life right now.

* Think like an artist: create instinctively and save revisions for later.

Start with your headlines, your current events. Your recent dreams most likely address these issues—although it is important to remember, of course, that dreams are multidimensional. Your dreams may have a literal meaning, a secondary meaning, a third meaning, and perhaps even a fourth, but you don't have to access them all at once. Always start by looking at how the dream, whatever it may be, relates to whatever is pressing most on your mind. Then create a dream scenario that speaks to these issues. Remember, in the dream world, there are no limits, no rules. And don't worry about filling in small details. These details will emerge instinctively and, when they do, they will be closer to the language of the unconscious, reflecting guidance in symbols much as in actual dreams.

Here, as an example, is a dream my friend (we'll call her "F") and I invented to help her understand what was going on in her present life—her mother's health. She was busy caring for her mother and making sure her prescriptions and appointments were in order. She was also really stressed out at work and experiencing conflicts with her boss. I started by setting the stage for her, then she took over.

DEC: You are walking down a street with a prescription for your mother's medications. For some reason, you have gotten out of your car and have to walk, and you find that the pharmacy is not where it usually is. You start looking around and wondering where it went. You can't find it, but you really need to get your mother her medications, so you stop others to ask for help or directions. No one knows where the pharmacy is; no one even seems to know what you're talking about. Take it from there.

F: I walk into the building where the pharmacy is supposed to be, but instead it's an amusement park with a huge Ferris wheel. I decide that, if I get on the Ferris wheel and go around a few times, maybe I'll find the pharmacy. When I get to the top, the wheel pauses, as Ferris wheels do. I look and, suddenly, there's a platform and the pharmacy is right there. I can just get off and walk across to it. Everything is up in the air.

DEC: If you could choose, would this be when you wake up or would the dream continue?

F: This is when I would wake up.

DEC: Now, let's go through the steps. Give the dream a title.

F: "Surprise."

DEC: Is the surprise pleasant or unpleasant?

F: Pleasant.

DEC: So what is the unconscious really saying? If you repeat what happens in your dream slowly, what do you learn? Then consider the meaning of the information by describing it to someone with no frame of reference. What is a prescription?

F: A way of getting medications that will improve my mother's, or someone's, health.

DEC: And how did you look for the medications?

F: I got out of my car. I had to walk, which took more effort. And the place that was supposed to supply what my mother needed was gone, so I had to ask for help to find it.

DEC: You ask for help and no one is able to help you. What then?

F: I look for the pharmacy in the building where it used to be. I go inside.

DEC: What is a pharmacy? And what did you find where it should have been?

F: A pharmacy is a place that is the source of something to help my mother, the place that has tools to make people well. There is a Ferris wheel where the pharmacy should be.

DEC: And what is a Ferris wheel?

F: It's a fun and gentle ride that brings people pleasure and amusement. It's very low key. It takes you way up in the air and then down again. You go around slowly, into and out of the sky.

DEC: And what do you do when you find the Ferris wheel, this gentle and amusing ride that takes you up into and brings you back down from the sky?

F: I decide to get on the Ferris wheel and enjoy it.

DEC: You don't cry or get hysterical or panic about where the medicine could be. Instead, you decide to have some fun. You ride the Ferris wheel and, lo and behold, you find the pharmacy at the top, up in the air. So, overall, what is the dream saying?

F: If I take the usual route to heal my mother, I may not find it. If I allow myself to relax, I will find a gentle and pleasurable way, with moments of lightness and joy, to support my mother's health.

DEC: And it will be up in the air; how amazing!

Inventing a dream can thus be another effective way of doing dreamwork. First, think about a current event in your life, something that is consuming your attention. Then make up a dream about it. Don't think about it; just take a basic situation related to your current life and let your imagination take over.

* You're on your way to work; you're running late; and then . . .

* You're making dinner for your family; and then . . .

When you create a dream in this way, you take something from your left-brain, logical waking world (the everyday situation or scenario) and imagine what might happen if that same event unfolded in a right-brain, symbolic world. You cross the bridge that separates your right brain and your left brain. But to become more adept at crossing the bridge, you need to go back and forth, back and forth, across it again and again. It's like learning a language; in order to become fluent, you need to practice.

When you invent a dream, you start out in the conscious world with whatever issue is uppermost in your mind, then cross the bridge into the unconscious. When the dream feels complete to you—that is, when you choose the point at which you want to wake up—you cross back into the conscious world with a message about what to do about your problem in waking life. For my friend, it was the revelation that bringing joy and delight to herself would, by extension, help her mother and be the most healing aspect of the experience. It was an amazing and beautifully supportive dream that she invented.

* * * * * * * * * * * * * * * *

To sum up...

1. Inventing a dream can be as useful as recalling one.

2. When you invent a dream, you take something from your left-brain, logical waking world and imagine the same situation in a right-brain, symbolic world.

3. When you invent a dream, always consider what is uppermost in your life right now.

4. When you invent a dream, think like an artist; create instinctively and save revisions for later.

CHAPTER 14

Working with Detailed Dreams

P eople who remember their dreams in great detail often ask me how they know where to start in analyzing them. When looking at a very detailed dream, it helps to focus on the details that were either the most dramatic—the most compelling to you personally—or those that were most out of synch with the rest of the dream—the alligator at the dinner table. "L" related a fairly detailed dream that illustrates how considering details individually and in relation to one another can help to translate a dream's message. Dreams may often seem "crazy" or completely nonsensical. This dream demonstrates how, with a little prodding, even the dreams that seem most bizarre make perfect sense if you look at them closely.

L: I had a dream last night that seems totally bizarre. I was a wizard and I went down this castle slide into a pool of filthy water that was just awful. They killed pigs in it and there were carcasses and pieces of garbage floating in the water. The castle was at Disney World, but it was also a real castle with a moat. I had to swim through the water, which was horribly muddy, murky, and stinky, and I was trying to keep my mouth above it so that I wouldn't drink it in. What does water mean in a dream?

DEC: It can mean many things. Describe water. Remember: I'm a Martian.

L: It is a liquid that we need to survive. You can travel on it or through it, but it can also drown you. It is used for both cleansing and recreation.

DEC: What qualities in life can carry you, can have you riding high, but can also drown you, cleanse you, and renew you? What can be wonderful and overwhelming in such a persistent, essential, and surrounding way?

L: Emotion?

DEC: Yes. Emotion is the life force; but emotions can also be overwhelming. So describe the water again, slowly, but keep in mind its connection to your emotional state.

L: The water was a mess. It was disgusting sludge and I really didn't want to get it in my mouth. You know, I've had a really bad week. I've been in pain, feeling down.

DEC: So it was disgusting because you felt you were immersed in a disgusting environment. Let's give the dream a title.

L: I really don't know what to call it. It was so disorienting, because it was as if I were at Disney World, but everything was too huge and realistic to be Disney World. The dream was so bizarre.

DEC: It is not bizarre; it is just condensed—like a picture conveying a thousand words. Don't overthink it. You're dreaming about yourself and, in your dream, you are a wizard at a castle in Disney World and you're sliding into a pool of filthy water. Title?

L: "Wizard at Disney World."

DEC: Okay. Now let's acknowledge what is uppermost in your life right now. You said you have been feeling low because your health is bad and you've had a rotten week. So that's what the dream is going to address. Now, describe what a wizard is.

L: A wizard is someone with magical powers, who can transform things using magic and alchemy.

DEC: In your dream, you are the wizard. You can transform things in the murky, disgusting water filled with carcasses. Transform them how? What is Disney World?

L: It is a bright and shiny amusement park. It's light-hearted, fun, playful.

DEC: So there are a number of messages in your dream. You feel you are sliding down, which is not like stepping slowly into a situation. It's swift and feels outside of your control. Remember— every part of the dream is important. You are sliding into the appalling water filled with dead animals, but you are also at Disney World, so there is an element of amusement there as well. If you look at it literally, it is disgusting and awful. This is particularly odd, because Disney is a clean place. But you are the wizard who can transform that foul water into something else in a situation that can be light-hearted and pleasant for you. How are you feeling about your environment in your waking life?

L: I'm feeling confused and taxed and just overwhelmed.

DEC: So in the dream, you feel as if you're barely keeping your head above water and have to keep the disgusting stuff out of your mouth. You're working hard to keep your head up. Where are you feeling so overwhelmed in your waking life? What problems are engulfing you? Remember that the dream dramatizes your waking experience in images.

L: I'm not sure.

DEC: Okay. Try digging deeper. What are pig carcasses?

L: A pig is an animal that eats slop, junk.

DEC: You are surrounded by dead pigs and the water is filled with garbage, which is what pigs eat. Apply this part to your waking life. Are you eating garbage in your waking life? Don't judge; just observe and embrace.

L: Yes.

DEC: And the pigs are dead in your dream. In other words, your unconscious may be telling you that you are eating slop during your waking hours and it is making you feel so unwell that it's overwhelming. But you can transform what you eat very easily, because you are a wizard—you have the power of transformation.

L: Actually, I remember that, in the dream, I was going to transform the water. It was almost peaceful. I was in the muck and it was so unpleasant, but I remember thinking: "I'm a wizard. I can change this water so that it is crystal clear and pure."

DEC: So maybe you are eating slop and it makes you feel messy, uncomfortable, and disgusting. The dream juxtaposes your stress and your sense of feeling overwhelmed with an amusement park, a place to play. So it's not only reporting on what is happening in your daily life; it is editorializing. It is pointing out that you can get out of this foul situation; you can transform it, and you can do so in a way that is pleasant and amusing.

L: That makes sense, because I kept thinking: "This is Disney World; it should just be perfect!" But the message is that I have to initiate the transformation.

DEC: The whole point is that you must do the work. But you don't want to do the work, do you?

L: I do and I don't.

DEC: That dilemma, that ambivalence, is represented in the dream. The dream is telling you that you are a wizard, but that, if you don't do the work, you end up drowning in the foul muck and feeling disgusted by it. What else is it telling you?

L: That if I do the work, I can transform it all.

DEC: And what other guidance is the dream giving you?

L: That I have to clarify my feelings. And the pigs send the message that I need to make some adjustments to transform the way I eat. I can't allow others to decide for me, because it's my life, my body, and I'm the one who will end up in the murky water.

This dream shows why it is so vital that we get to a point where we avoid having knee-jerk reactions to our dreams or seeing them as just crazy or bizarre, totally nonsensical. What is Disney World? It is a big and fascinating place, and there are magical characters and settings there. It's really that simple. We just get lost because we haven't yet become fluent in the language of symbols.

* * * * * * * * * * * * * * * * *

To sum up...

1. Even the dreams that seem most bizarre make perfect sense when you look at them closely.

2. When you interpret very detailed dreams, focus on the details that were either the most dramatic or those that were most out of synch with the rest of the dream.

3. Even very complex dreams always relate back to a situation or event in your waking life.

CHAPTER 15

Working with
Multiple Dreams

S everal dreams can illuminate and inform one another. The dreams do not have to be from the same night or even the same year. Because there is no time in the unconscious, a decades-old dream that occurs to you now may have a meaningful connection to a dream from the previous night.

The dreams that "E" describes below are especially helpful in illustrating this, because the dreamer is very left-brained and literal in his waking life, but is making great progress in using his right-brained, intuitive side. In other words, he is like most people in that his inclination is to approach things with logic. However, like anyone reading this book, he is interested in developing his understanding of the unconscious. He described his most recent dream like this:

E: In the dream, everyone at work had to learn about and take turns cleaning up an extrusion line and it came to be my turn.

DEC: What is an extrusion line; what is its function? Remember that you are explaining this to a Martian. Extrusion means to take away, to pull something out. In your engineering work, is that what it means?

E: It means a line for making a product.

DEC: Can you be more specific? A line for making what kind of product?

E: Tubing. The importance, I think, of the dream is that I had cleaned extrusion lines before, so I convinced them I didn't have to do the training. Since I do it all the time, I didn't need to prove anything.

DEC: Were the others practicing this function in the dream? And how many were there?

E: The other people were not important.

DEC: Remember—just observe and embrace. Don't attempt to decide what is and is not important. There is information in every part of a dream. Right now, we are just gathering data. Can you estimate how many people were there? Don't overthink it; just say the first number that comes to your head.

E: Two, other than myself. When the dream ended, I didn't have to learn about or clean the line because I already knew how to do it. That is what the dream was about.

DEC: So the other engineers do not get out on the floor with the operators, but you get down to the nitty-gritty. You did not need to do the training, because you are an expert. You are more experienced.

E: Yes, I think it means that I am more experienced.

DEC: Okay. Can you give your dream a title?

E: "Training."

DEC: And what is the dream really saying?

E: It's telling me that I know what I'm doing now, and don't have to prove myself.

DEC: Yes. You don't need to do the basics anymore; you can move on to another level. But remember that dreams are multidimensional. So at the literal level, your dream is saying something about work, where you've already mastered the basics. Now let's carry that to other levels in your waking life Are extrusions something you taught yourself how to do?

E: I learned over time, by trial and error and hands-on experience.

DEC: Okay, wonderful. Let's apply this to everyday life. Your dream is saying that you have been training and doing certain things and you have become a whole lot better through practice. Where in your life do you feel you need training? Where in your life do you feel skilled and capable? Start with the most basic things.

E: One thing is spiritual readings.

DEC: In waking life, you don't feel you need additional training in providing spiritual readings, because you've worked at that skill, practiced it, done it, and found that you are good at it. Tell me more.

E: I think the dream is reassuring me that I have been doing readings successfully, that I know how to do them, and can stop worrying about it.

DEC: So it is telling you to have more confidence and self-esteem. Remember, *your* dream was engineered by an engineer who is very left-brained, very technical and work oriented.

At this point in our conversation, I noticed that E was rubbing his knee. Remember that we talked about this earlier in the context of masculine and feminine energies. But the action becomes even more significant when seen in the context of this dream. So I pointed it out.

DEC: Why do you keep rubbing your knee?

E: Oh, it's nothing.

DEC: No, this is important. Don't exclude things. Ask yourself why you are rubbing your knee, because the body also speaks symbolically. For instance, are you rubbing your left or right knee?

E: Left.

DEC: And the left side of the body is feminine energy—the energy of all the women in your life. Your feminine energy involves your intuition, your creativity, so this relates to your spiritual readings—your intuition. Discussing this has made you feel a bit restless, and that has to do with your intuition as well. What do you want to do with your intuition?

E: Spiritual readings.

DEC: And your unconscious is telling you that you do not need additional training—at least that was your interpretation of the suggestion for your waking life. But you are feeling restless about it—rubbing your knee as you speak of it—which is your body's way of communicating that you have been feeling restless about your intuition.

I let him think about that for a moment. We would return to the meaning of this restless bodily response shortly. But for now, I brought the discussion back to the dream elements.

DEC: What is tubing at its most basic level?

E: A conduit; a channel or vehicle.

DEC: Do you see the symbolism? When you are doing psychic work, what are you doing? You are acting as a tube, a conduit, a channel for spiritual information. If we put the two together, the dream and your waking life, there is direct applicability. Now let's go back to your restlessness, because that is a further application of the dream. Talk about what is standing in your way and what is holding you back.

E: I am afraid to tell people what I do.

DEC: Out of fear? Shame? Embarrassment?

E: Embarrassment. I worry about what people will think.

DEC: Okay, let's apply that reaction even more deeply to your life. What is the first number that comes into your mind when you say you are embarrassed, afraid to tell people?

E: Zero.

DEC: And what does zero represent? The smallest quantity? The origin? By extension, perhaps a baby? Perhaps the dream is telling you that the only thing holding you back is fear of the past— maybe you know; maybe you don't know. After all, at zero, at the very beginning, as a baby, you don't know or remember anything. But it doesn't matter.

At this point, I encouraged E to be in the present, to take a deep breath, exhale, and imagine treating himself in the same supportive and loving way that he would treat his own children—to tell the infant in himself that he is loved and supported and that he is amazing. Then to come back as a full-grown adult who can acknowledge the source of his fear and restlessness.

DEC: You are feeling restless about your work, which your unconscious is saying you have already sufficiently mastered—both
your work as an engineer and your spiritual work. But you are
feeling restless because you want to do more of this work. This
opens the door to making a change in your conscious life. So
how does feeling embarrassed about your spiritual work hold
you back? Understanding this will help you to move forward
and do more spiritual work.

E: I am afraid of people saying I'm crazy, that I can't do readings.

DEC: All right. Can you attach a number to that fear?

E: Ten.

DEC: And what was going on in your life when you were ten?

E: My mother and brother were in the hospital being treated for
mental disorders.

DEC: And you were afraid that they would send you away as well.
See how looking at a dream in layers and applying it to different aspects of your life can be so revealing? You are more
confident in your daily and spiritual work; you don't need to
prove yourself any longer. However, you are feeling restless
because you are not allowing yourself to pursue that work to
your full abilities because you are afraid people will believe you
are crazy or not capable of intuition and spiritual reading.

E: Ah, I see.

Then we moved on to another dream E had recently had. I asked
him to recall it and give me a brief summary of its narrative. He told of
a dream in which he had to reset something on a piece of equipment to
ensure that his life worked out right. But for whatever reason, he found he
didn't have to hit the "reset" button. He seemed confused by the dream
and said it didn't make sense to him. I told him that was quite common.

Then I pointed out to him that it was the second time that week that he had spoken of a dream in the context of machinery, of work, of engineering. That seemed significant, so I asked him to go a little further.

DEC: What is the theme of this dream?

E: That things in my life will work out without my needing to hit "reset."

DEC: And what does "reset" mean? How does resetting a machine apply to your everyday life?

E: It means to start over. But I don't need to do it.

DEC: What don't you need to start over in your life? How does this apply to your waking life?

Again, E seemed confused and unsure, so I prompted him.

DEC: What do you engage in on a daily basis? Your waking life involves your marriage, your family, your job, your friends, your children. Let's look at each of these areas—systematically, as an engineer would—to identify where you feel you may be concerned about starting over.

E: I don't think I need to start over at work. I can continue where I am, because work is going well.

DEC: That fits very nicely, but it's not just that. Remember, dreams are multidimensional—their meaning has one layer after another layer after another. What is your unconscious saying about other areas in your life? Who else was in the dream and where was it set?

E: I was at work. There were other people, but no one I knew.

DEC: That's not uncommon.

E: As for other areas in my life, I guess I take this dream as generally positive.

DEC: It's not a good idea to judge a dream as positive or negative. But tell me what you think the message of this positive dream is.

E: To me, it means that I am on the right path.

DEC: So it's supportive. But if the dream were trying to shake you up, to give you some information or a warning, would that be negative?

E: No, although it would be uncomfortable.

DEC: Well, yes, it's always more pleasant to get positive feedback. But let's go beyond what is simply positive feedback. Apply the message to other areas in your life.

E: Okay. I guess it could be trying to tell me that I'm pushing things more, in a good way, with my wife. I know I have been. There are things she has wanted me to do and sometimes I let her win. But lately, I've pushed back.

DEC: That is important, because that is where you've had the most resistance, the most difficulty. So your dream isn't just about work. It is also about your life at home, where progress has always been the most difficult for you. Tell me what happened.

E: My wife was upset about a few things I was planning to do and I didn't give her the chance to argue with me. I just told her I was doing them, and that was that.

I reminded him that, when you're connecting a dream to your daily life, it helps to be very specific and include details. The details can be very revealing. Then I suggested that he tell me more.

E: I just told her I was going and I would be back in a reasonable amount of time. I didn't care whether she liked it or not. After all, she goes and does the things she wants to do and I don't stop her. So I just made up my mind to do the same.

DEC: Yes, and that is very significant for you.

E: Yes. But I respected her, too, by telling her when I was going to be back. I did what I wanted to do because she does, and I've realized that it's not really right for her to tell me I can't do something when she does whatever she wants. But I still respected her.

DEC: And this kind of exchange reflects an adult response, as opposed to a child requesting permission. So, regarding your waking life, the dream is telling you on one level that you don't have to hit "reset" at work, but on another level, a deeper level, it is also saying that you don't have to keep repeating an established pattern. Specifically, you do not have to continue asking for permission just because it is what you have done in the past, and you don't have to start all over again either. You can simply decide to change your response to the situation and proceed from where you are now. You don't have to go back and reset the machinery. You don't have to repeat that particular pattern, whether with your wife or something that is standing in for her.

I pointed out to him that the value of his dream was that it showed him that the path he was on was a good one. It's working out; it's fine. He doesn't have to change jobs; he can continue on the way he has been; he doesn't have to reset the machinery. So this one little image had tremendous relevance for him when he applied it to what he was doing in his waking life. That's when he could begin to see its value.

Then we started to explore how this dream applied to the rest of his family.

DEC: Your children are very important people in your life; can you apply it to them? What's happening at home? Have there been any changes?

E: Mostly my kids worry about my health and want me to lose weight. They get mad if I eat too much. I'm a terrible nibbler at night. During the day, I don't eat much, but at night, I tend to snack. But honestly, I don't see how this dream connects with my son and daughter.

DEC: It may just be a comment that you don't need to reset the way you're interacting with them. Your relationship with them is strong. What comes up when you apply this dream to friends?

E: I don't have problems with any of my friends.

DEC: Good. So if you could change the dream in any way, how would you change it?

E: I wouldn't change anything, because I see it as very positive, meaning I can go on with my life because things are working out better every day.

DEC: And how can you enhance what you're doing? Remember, life is about change; it's about motion, movement. Nothing in life is static. How can this dream guide you to improve your life? If you assume a dream or symbol has no guidance to offer you, that everything is fine exactly the way it is, you may miss something that could make your life even better.

E: Well, I guess I could be more open and talkative with my wife. I could try to understand what she is communicating to me before jumping to conclusions.

DEC: Yes, but how would you do this without hitting that "reset" button? Your dream relates to circumstances at work and at home. So it's really trying to encourage you to see how what you're doing in one context can help you make different choices, different decisions, in the other. It's supportive.

I reminded E that sometimes your unconscious tries to shake you up, as in a nightmare. It tries to wake you up, both literally and metaphorically, and tell you that you need to pay attention and make changes. And sometimes it just wants to tell you that you're doing fine and to keep up the good work. But what it's really saying, in either case, is that the single most important thing for you is to express that adult part of yourself, your higher self—your qualities, your judgment, your decisions. Then I asked him if he remembered any older dreams—from a year ago, or even thirty years ago.

E: I remember a dream I had years ago in which I'm making love to somebody; I don't even know who she is.

DEC: Describe the dream.

E: We're making love—it's just kissing, but it's very good. That's as much as I remember.

DEC: Apply it to what was happening in your life at that time. When did you have the dream?

E: It was probably at a time when my wife and I were fighting a lot, probably not talking much.

DEC: So it may have been portraying the hope or the desire that you had to return to a more loving relationship. You were kissing in the dream; you were close in the dream; you were comfortable; you felt good about the connection. But remember, the dreamer is always dreaming about the dreamer. So when you were dreaming about making love with this woman, you were also dreaming about the current events in your waking life at a time when your connection with your wife was not very good. And the desire and the wish was about being close to a female, to a woman, in a way that was loving and supportive. You were yearning for something you were missing.

E: Yes, that's the way I took it back when I had the dream. I tell you, in the dream, it felt so real.

DEC: Yes, and because it felt so good, you probably wanted to go back and live it again. Let's talk about that. What do you do in this dream that you are either doing or not doing in your waking life? You are kissing—you're showing affection with your mouth, which also represents speaking.

E: And speaking—communicating—is something I wasn't doing very well at that time.

DEC: There you go. The dream was telling you that, in waking life, if you communicated better, you could more easily connect with a woman in your life. It wasn't just wishful thinking. Your unconscious was offering guidance. It was telling you that, if you expressed more of yourself—with your mouth, your words, your affection—you would have a more positive response in your waking life. What do you need to do to achieve this? Describe it.

E: If I want more affection in my life, I have to communicate with my wife more affectionately—versus accusing, fighting, whatever.

DEC: Okay, now let's return to the present, because the past dream you just brought up has relevance, because it was your unconscious that brought it up.

E: My unconscious?

I explained that his unconscious was urging him to pay attention to this dream in the context of his present life. The two dreams were directly connected. One was telling him to be more assertive and stand up for himself; the other was telling him to speak up more sweetly and with more affection. If he did both, he would have a better outcome. Then I urged him to get into specifics.

DEC: What can you do in your waking life to apply the guidance from these dreams?

E: I'll have to be more conscientious and remind myself to speak up for myself, but to do so gently and affectionately. And I need to show my wife that I care about her more often.

DEC: Good. Now be specific. Break it down.

E: I have to remind myself daily to say one or two caring and affectionate things.

DEC: Yes. You need to condition yourself to have good emotional habits, as well as good physical habits. Just as you have learned to brush your teeth every day, you have to pay attention to your emotional hygiene every day. Help yourself to do this by connecting the action to a time when you're at home doing something habitual, or on your regular way home from work. This can help you remind yourself to do what you need to do.

E: On my way home every day, I can think about it and remind myself to say something nice. And I can give her a kiss on the cheek.

DEC: Wonderful. Now do you begin to see the relevance of these dreams? Do you see how connected they are.

E: Yes, yes.

When E applied the warmth, the good feeling, from his remembered dream to his present life, he realized that he had chosen his wife as his partner, and had chosen to remain with her. His dream was simply telling him to re-create some of that warmth in his relationship with her. Next, I asked him about his childhood.

DEC: You did not have that warmth growing up, did you?

E: No.

DEC: And what a wonderful expression of your personal growth that you're beginning to create it in your current life, even though you didn't have it as a child. Now do you see the value of applying the dreams?

E: The value is that dreams highlight parts of your life in which you're doing a good job—and tell you why—and also show you parts of your life you need to work on—and tell you how. So for me, I'm doing a good job of communicating more at work and at home, and now I have to be more affectionate and more expressive of my feelings—which I don't do.

DEC: No—which you haven't done *yet*. If you say that you don't do something, you just continue the energy of the issue your dream is trying to point out to you. Your two dreams are telling you that you've made wonderful changes and now it is time to "connect from the mouth." That's why you remembered the kissing dream. Of all the dreams you had, that's the one you remembered, recalling how good it was to be loving with that woman. Moreover the unconscious is telling you that you can communicate not only with the woman outside of yourself, but also with the feminine energy within yourself. At the point in your life when you had that dream, you started opening up very significantly—to your unconscious, to past lives, to achieving, and to communicating with your higher self. All of that is feminine energy, not masculine energy—not the engineer. It is the energy of the healer, the intuitive, the one who is communicating completely at other levels.

Always try to apply your dreams to all the important areas of your life, in different layers, and in different situations in your life. You live in your house, you live in your work, you live in your marriage, with your children, with your family, with your friends. So you need to apply the messages offered in your dreams to all these important aspects of your life. A dream from years ago, if you remember it today, has relevance because there is no time in the unconscious. What happened twenty years ago is relevant today, just as it was to what happened twenty years ago.

Think of the unconscious as a large stadium. In a stadium, everything is out in the open. You can see everything that is going on. And if you have binoculars that magnify what you see or earphones that magnify what you hear, you can hear and see everything that's going on all at once—the past, the present, and the future. Because it's not sequential, it's all out there *now*. So when you recall a dream that took place twenty years ago, your unconscious is telling you that you need to think about that dream, because it adds another layer of meaning to your current life.

* * * * * * * * * * * * * * * * *

To sum up...

1. Working with the symbols from a past dream can show you how it relates to situations in your life when you had the dream.

2. Applying the combined messages and guidance from multiple dreams can help you enhance your present everyday life.

3. There is no time in the unconscious, so dreams from the past are as relevant now as they were at the time you had them.

4. When your unconscious brings up a past dream, it is telling you that it is relevant to your present dreams and to situations in your conscious life.

Part IV

Interpreting
Your Own Dreams

CHAPTER 16

Getting Started

I n this section, we are going to work with your dreams. If you are eager to get started, but have not yet recalled or recorded a dream, you can follow the steps for inventing a dream scenario discussed in chapter 13 and expanded on in chapter 17.

The questions and suggestions given here are only a guide to get you started. This is not homework, nor is it meant to be a program you must follow. The key is to keep things simple, so do not feel that you have to answer every question or even access every layer of a dream. If the process becomes unwieldy, you won't stick with it. Rather, these suggestions are meant to get you started, to give you a nudge. As you continue to work with your dreams, you will find the seven steps easier and easier to follow. Eventually, they will become nearly effortless, instinctive.

When you begin, set a goal that you can meet. I recommend trying to work with three dreams per week. Set a goal; write it down; revisit it as you work. You have to set goals so that you can mark your progress. Otherwise, although you may make yourself feel better in the short term, you won't have the tools you need to make substantive changes in your life, and you will do no lasting good. In order to accomplish anything of worth, you have to do the work.

There are four key elements to remember as you move through the seven steps:

* The dreamer is always dreaming about the dreamer, so your dreams are always about *you.*

* Like a newspaper, dreams report and editorialize on events in your current everyday life.

* Do not overthink your reactions; just go with whatever comes to mind first.

* Be patient; skill is achieved through practice.

As you work through these steps, you can use the worksheet given at the end of this chapter to record your reactions and responses. Or you can just use a plain pad of paper to keep track of your thoughts.

First, jot down a summary of a dream. It can be a recent dream, or a dream from your past. Remember, dreams from the past that come to mind now, no matter how long ago you had them, will have direct relevance to your current waking life because they are brought forward by your unconscious.

Give your dream a title—the first thing that comes to mind. Reread aloud what you have written, very slowly. Then answer quickly: What is uppermost in your everyday life right now? If you are working with an older dream, consider what was going on in your life at the time that you had the dream.

If you are having trouble thinking of a situation in your present life, try answering the following questions. Use the context of the time period in which you had the dream if you are working with a dream from the past.

* What is/was going on at work? Have you taken on any new responsibilities or projects? Do you enjoy your job and the people you work with? Do you feel you have time enough for the non-work-related areas of your life?

* How are/were things going in your primary relationships? Include family—children, spouse, parents, siblings, other relations—friends, acquaintances, colleagues, and pets.

* How do/did you assess your situation in terms of your finances, physical health, emotional health, social life, and sex life?

* If you had total control over your life, are/were there any changes you would make? If so, what?

* Have any major changes recently taken place, or do you anticipate major changes in the immediate future?

Next, list the objects, characters, and settings in the dream. If the dream is brief, you can address each item. If the dream is very detailed, or you are simply short on time, just note the details that seem most significant to you. These may be the details you remember in the most vivid detail, or the ones that seem most out of place. For instance, if you dreamed you were in your home, but there was a large painting on the wall that is not there in your actual house, that may be a place to start.

Now describe each item or element as if you were talking to a Martian. Belabor the obvious, describing things literally and then considering what other meanings may be attached to them. Some examples:

* A rose is a flower, the brightly colored and fragrant top of a plant. It can also be a symbol of love—specifically, romantic love. People send their beloved bouquets of roses as a sign of affection.

* A cat is a small animal that many people keep in their homes as a pet. It is also a symbol of mystery and wile. Cats have historically been associated with the Divine and with feminine energy.

* An infant is a newborn human. It is helpless and completely dependent on others for survival. A newborn is considered innocent and often brings people joy; its arrival is something people celebrate.

* Eating involves taking in food to nourish the body and provide it with energy. It can be a pleasurable experience or a bad one. Eating is universal among humans and necessary for survival. We eat to fill our stomachs.

Summarize the message the dream is sending from the unconscious. It may be helpful to think about the dream as a children's story or a parable. If your dream were a story, what would its moral be? Again, don't overthink it. If you've followed the steps, you probably already have a strong sense of what your unconscious may be saying. Don't analyze; just note it on your worksheet or paper.

Consider the dream's guidance for your waking life. Look back over your notes and see if the dream has offered any suggestions for addressing your major concerns. Remember, however, that, because some dreams are more about calling your attention to a problem than solving it, it may be up to you to determine what steps you can take to respond to the message from your unconscious. Either way, begin by noting what you believe the dream is guiding you to do.

Reflecting on this guidance, list some specific steps you can take to accomplish your ends. That is, if your dream is guiding you to be more expressive with your affection, list one or two actual steps you can take to be more expressive. Remember, this shouldn't be a burdensome task; just focus on simple steps that accomplish your ends and make sure they are easily achievable. If your dream is warning you that you are eating poorly and your health may suffer, promise to eat one piece of fruit every day. Over time, the behaviors you practice will become habitual. As you progress, you can challenge yourself further. But at the beginning, focus on what's simple and achievable, and the results will motivate you to go on from there. Return to your notes periodically to see if you are keeping up.

Remember, you do not have to use this worksheet to follow the steps, but it may prove helpful as you begin learning them. Whatever is easiest for you to accommodate in your waking life is what you are most likely to continue.

* * * * * * * * * * * * * * * * * *

To sum up...

1. Be spontaneous; don't overthink; just observe and embrace.

2. Jot down a summary of your dream and give it a title.

3. Relate your dream to what is uppermost in your life at the time.

4. List the objects, characters, and settings in your dream.

5. Summarize your dream's message.

6. Consider the relevance of your dream's message for your waking life.

7. List specific steps you can take to follow the guidance offered by your dream.

8. Be patient and persistent; skill comes with practice.

Worksheet

Goal: _____

_____

_____

Summary: _____

_____

_____

Title: _____

Relevance to life: _____

_____

_____

Dream objects/characters/settings: _____

_____

Summary of the message: _____

_____

_____

_____

Dream guidance: _____

_____

Steps to accomplish the ends: _____

_____

CHAPTER 17

Creating
Dream Scenarios

A s you practice your nighttime ritual of stating that you will remember and record your dreams, and your morning ritual of quickly jotting down what you recall of them, you will have more and more dreams and details with which to work. In the meantime, however, or during times when you are struggling to remember dreams, you can invent a dream to continue with your dreamwork. The steps below will help you create a dream scenario that is as revealing as one experienced during sleep.

There are three key elements to remember as you create your dream scenario:

* Choose a scenario related to whatever is most on your mind today.

* Don't overthink it; the dream doesn't have to "make sense" in terms of your logical left brain.

* Let your imagination guide you across the bridge between consciousness and the unconscious.

Again, you can use the worksheet from chapter 16 or just a plain piece of paper to record your imagined dream. The important thing is to be systematic in how you go about inventing the dream scenario and meticulous in how you record it.

First, think about what is currently going on in your life; what is consuming your attention. Note a few of the details on your worksheet or paper, then choose a scenario based on those situations. For instance, if you've written down that you are concerned about your spouse's health, you may begin the dream by imagining that you are driving him or her to a medical appointment. Speak aloud or jot down your dream narrative in just a few words, with as little editing as possible. Don't overthink it. Don't judge. Whatever comes to mind, just go with it. Then let your imagination take over.

The everyday rules of the logical, left-brained world do not apply here. You may be driving one minute and flying the next; you may find yourself able to run very fast or barely able to move at all; you may be making love to someone you've never met, even if that's something you would never do in waking life. When you create a dream in this way, you take something from your left-brained, logical universe and imagine what might happen if the same events were to unfold in a right-brained, symbolic universe. You cross the bridge that separates your right brain from your left brain. In order to become skilled at crossing the bridge, you need to practice, going back and forth again and again.

Decide at what point you want your dream to stop. When do you want to wake up? Are you in a pleasurable or an upsetting situation? Do you feel amused, threatened, comforted, fearful? Considering where you are and how you feel when you wake up—or, in this case, discontinue the narrative—will guide your understanding of the dream.

Using your invented dream, proceed through the seven steps of dream exploration. If you need a little help getting started, try this abbreviated exercise. Quickly answer these questions about a hypothetical dream in which you are having sex with someone from your past:

* Who is it?

* What did that person represent to you at that point in your life?

* What is uppermost in your life right now?

* What is your unconscious saying to you? With which qualities does it suggest you need to experience intimacy?

If you proceed without self-editing, instinctively, the few details and words you add to the scenario will be a perfect reflection of the themes and issues affecting your daily life and the recommendations coming from the unconscious, because the first thing that occurs to you is always from your unconscious. If you respond before considering—before engaging your left brain—you may be surprised at the details or words you choose to describe something. As long as you proceed without second-guessing yourself, your descriptions will be very revealing.

With this technique, you begin in the conscious world with a specific issue and create a "dream" through which you cross into the unconscious—while awake. When the dream is complete, you return to the conscious world carrying a message from the unconscious. Whatever that message may be, it will hold amazing insight and information concerning what to do about your problems in waking life. By acting on these insights, you can begin to manifest the changes you long to make in yourself, your life, and the world that you inhabit.

* * * * * * * * * * * * * * * * *

To sum up...

1. Choose a scenario related to what is uppermost in your everyday life.

2. Note a few details of the scenario on a worksheet or piece of paper in as few words as possible.

3. Don't overthink or edit your dream narrative.

4. Let your imagination take over and carry you across the bridge from your conscious mind to your unconscious.

5. Apply the seven steps of dream exploration to your imagined dream.

CHAPTER 18

Reentering Dreams

A s you progress in your dreamwork, you may wish to reenter and reexperience or alter a particular dream. The technique of reentering and altering a dream is only useful, however, after you have a clear sense of what the unconscious has been trying to tell you. If you change a dream before you have received its true message, it will just keep knocking at the door, louder and louder. Thus, before you proceed, make sure you have considered the following questions:

* How is the dream related to current events, to today's date and time?

* How are you feeling in your conscious world, in your everyday life?

* What are you observing and what is really uppermost in your mind when you are awake?

Remember to think like a newspaper editor. The headlines only address the most pressing issues of the day. The editorials offer comparisons—how what is occurring today differs from previous occurrences—and recommendations. Once you have worked with your dream, have understood its message, and have addressed what it is telling you, you can make any changes you want.

First, select a dream that you want to change or transform and allow yourself to enter a gentle trance. To induce this state, take three deep breaths, breathing in through your nose, holding the breath for four seconds, and exhaling through your mouth. Your exhalation should be longer than your inhalation. When you exhale, do not purse your lips as if you were pushing out the air. Simply drop your jaw and exhale, making a sound like "Hahhhhh."

Enter the dream with all of your senses activated. With your eyes, note what is going on, what colors are present. Is the dream in black and white? Is the setting dark or light? With your nose, determine if there are any smells in the dream. Are you passing by a bakery and smelling bread? With your ears, listen for sounds. What do you hear? Is anything being said? What sounds are you or anyone else making? What sounds are nearby, if any? Is there complete silence?

Be aware of the characters in the dream and their actions. Notice your feelings in response to those actions. Then begin a dialog with each character. Ask them all why they are there and what they want to tell you. Tell them whatever you need to in order to transform the dream.

Finally, transform and rewrite the dream in any way that you want. Allow your imagination to take flight and rewrite whatever comes into your awareness, whichever way you want it to go.

* * * * * * * * * * * * * * * * * *

To sum up...

1. Select the dream you want to transform. Make sure it is a dream whose message you already understand.

2. Enter a gentle trance by taking three deep breaths.

3. Enter the dream with all your senses activated—eyes, ears, nose.

4. Dialog with each character in the dream and tell them how you want to change it.

5. Rewrite the dream however your imagination dictates.

CONCLUSION:
THE POWER OF CHOICE

When I began writing, I felt so inept. I had to audio record everything in my first book—*Repetition: Past Lives, Life and Rebirth* (Hay House, 2008)—because, for me, writing it needed to be an interactive experience. I had to discuss my ideas with a living person who could respond and challenge me, motivating me to be clearer and simpler, pushing me closer to my goal. As I questioned my abilities, I had a dream whose message reassured me that, although I felt inept, my work had value and importance. I am so grateful to have received that message, because it is important to me to share this information with as many people as possible to help them wake up to the rich possibilities of the unconscious.

Although I felt compelled to write this book, I exercised free choice by getting started despite the challenges I knew I would face. We exercise free choice consciously and unconsciously, and this is why it is so important to learn the language of the unconscious through working with your dreams. Too often, we disown our free choice, believing instead in fate, or destiny, or the irresistable influence of the past. We blame parents, or events, or circumstances seemingly beyond our control for the paths we take. But, in truth, our lives are shaped by our choices, and, whether we exercise this freedom consciously or unconsciously, we may as well embrace and own it. When we do not, we extend our confusion and unhappiness.

In *As You Like It*, Shakespeare says that life is a play, and that all men are merely actors on its stage. What he fails to see, however, is you are the director, the producer, and the author of the play, as well as its main actor. It is all *your* story. If you sit in the audience and do not claim the story as your own, you will be powerless to do anything about it if the story takes a turn you do not like

Indeed, terrible things do happen. But if you exercise your free will, there will always be something you can do about them. I prefer to put my energy not into preparing for the worst—for instance, hoarding cans and sacks of rice in a fallout shelter somewhere—but rather in praying for change. After the oil spill in the Gulf, I did not assume that the environment was doomed. Instead, I prayed that the Gulf would gurgle again with blue water and oxygen and fish. That is what I want, because I believe that everything in God's world is a two-way street—everything seeks equilibrium. If you go crazy, you can also become sane. You gain weight; you can lose it. You get ill; you can become healthy. Everything can be changed. This is why it is so important to embrace your nightmares as well as your gentler, more pleasant dreams. Try to think of nightmares as proof that your body loves you so much that it sends jolts to wake you up. If you do not become aware of your own fears and obstacles, you cannot do anything to control them and will continue to live in fear.

Living in fear is in direct opposition to a healthy life and what the Divine wants for us. When we walk in fear, we become constricted and "constipated" at all levels. Opening up to joy and finding beauty in the smallest details and in the magnificence of nature make it possible to accept and embrace divine love. Further, these reminders help to restore the balance I speak about so often. Peace and joy and beauty *will* help to balance the stress, the speed, and the hectic nature of our typical waking lives.

The unconscious, the dream world, makes up 95 percent of our awareness. Moreover, there is no time or place in the unconscious. So in dreams, we can be in one place or in 10,000 places at the same time. In our physical bodies, we can only be in one place at a time. You can project your voice or tape it to send it somewhere else, but you can only physically be in one place while inhabiting that paltry 5 percent of your reality that is your conscious life.

In the unconscious, time collapses. There is no distinction between past, present, or future. That is why, while I believe in projections, I do not believe in predictions. A projection conveys a sense that something *may* happen—maybe in a month; maybe in ten months; maybe not at all. The unconscious makes statements from a place where there is no time, so trying to impose a definitive timeline on its messages is not relevant or helpful. A projection is a suggestion of what *may* be, not a statement of what *will* be. Such statements are distortions of a far more complex and important part of our relationship as souls in a larger reality.

If you are attentive, your dreams may signal that there may be an opportunity in coming months for you to meet someone who will become important to you. That makes it your responsibility to pursue that possibility. The projection will, or will not, come to pass based on what you choose to do. If you take no action, it is very unlikely that the possibility will be realized. Thus the unconscious does not counter, but rather reinforces, one of God's most profound and basic gifts—free choice.

Dreams are really all about exercising that free choice and making changes in the conscious world. The unconscious determines the vast majority of your behavior, and when you make the unconscious conscious, you create a bridge. We tend to be attentive to nightmares because they grab our attention; they are intense and memorable. But all dreams are giving you messages. Our left brains are connected to our right brains; our consciousness is connected to our unconscious. Yet, we disown it. Our dreams seem crazy because we interpret them as if they speak the language of the conscious world. If you grow up speaking English and hear people speaking Chinese, it sounds totally incomprehensible, when in fact it is a language as full and rich as your own. It is just that you do not know and understand it.

Dreams are the same. When we stop calling our dreams crazy, we take judgment out of the equation. You are not neurotic or psychotic if you have disturbing dreams, whether or not they recur. There is nothing wrong with you. You are likely just repeating patterns in your everyday life that do not serve you, and your unconscious is offering you guidance to help you exit those patterns.

Everybody dreams. And yet, our dreams are so personal—a unique reflection of our own identities. Some say we must suppress this ego identity, but I find this an artificial and unnecessary separation. That may work and be crucial for certain spiritual practitioners, but most of us are not able to spend our days meditating in the safety of an ashram, being fed and having the requirements of our daily lives met. Most of us are just out in the world, living our lives. We must get to know the ego and not make an enemy of it. You have to have a sense of self. If you don't, then you enter the world of the unconscious untethered, unconnected to anything. This is how we often feel about the dream world.

Remember the analogy of the dream world as a stadium. When you enter the stadium, you may not immediately know where your seat is. You may not even know what game is being played. It is totally overwhelming. The most important thing in navigating that space is to know yourself, and you cannot know yourself if you have no sense of your own ego—your identity in the conscious world. How can you survive real life if you do not know who you are?

The whole point of working with dreams is to learn how to enter the unconscious—both tethered and untethered. When you enter the stadium with a ticket, you are tethered to a section, a row, a seat. You have some structure, some guidelines, some points of reference from the left brain that are logical and sequential. These help you enter the stadium—that is, help you cross the bridge to the unconscious—with some sense of direction. You feel more anchored and are able to orient yourself. And this is important, because we all need some direction, some predictability. Once you are seated, you can begin to take in everything around you and begin to access the richness of your dreams. You can begin to make the 95 percent of your unconscious accessible to your conscious 5 percent.

Learning a new technique is always somewhat awkward. But remember that your dreamwork can be completed in just a couple of minutes at a time, at convenient points during the day. Keep it quick and easy so that it does not become a burdensome task that you will not maintain. The process is simple and straightforward; you want to get to the heart of your dreams' messages quickly and efficiently so you can begin to change destructive patterns in your life. When you enter the unconscious and begin communicating in the language of symbols, you also want to make sure that you can cross the bridge back into the conscious world again. After all, you live in the conscious world, and the value of your work with the unconscious is that it allows you to return to your daily life and manage your everyday responsibilities better. Crossing the bridge from conscious life to the unconscious and returning enriches your life. And when you enrich your own life, you enrich humanity as a whole.

When you learn to cross the bridge between consciousness and the unconscious easily, you gain a wonderful freedom. Once you are able to do it, you can enter the unconscious whenever you like—a place where there are no limitations. You are free to take a wide array of incredible journeys, and yet return to the here and now to pursue your waking life. Best of all, your souvenirs from the journey will be more enlightenment, fascination, delight, and, most important, the vital guidance that your dreams can deliver.

The best way to get started is to set simple and plain expectations. Begin with just one or two dreams a week. Over time, aim for three. What will motivate you to continue and to work with even more dreams is how quickly and clearly you will be able to understand so much more about your life. That is what you are really trying to achieve. And you can do it easily if you just find the few minutes it takes. Nightmares and recurring dreams will be the sharpest and will tug at you the most, so if there are any that have stayed with you for some time, begin there. But no matter where you begin—just begin.

All the work we do on dreams involves entering the unconscious, where communication takes place in the language of symbolsm, imagery, and creativity. And this language constitutes 95 percent of our behaviors. When you begin to connect your dreams to one another—over several weeks or even years—you may find that your dreams address the same themes over and over. If this is the case for you, it means that you are trying to heal from themes and issues that you have not yet successfully addressed. Dreams and the unconscious can help you face those issues and make important decisions and choices for yourself and your life. It is such a waste if you ignore this rich resource.

One of the reasons that the *Harry Potter* books are so popular is that they are set in a school. In a sense, the books show us that magic is something we can study, practice, and learn ourselves. The same is true with dreamwork. If you do not immediately understand the message of your dreams—if they are not totally clear and simple at first—just remember that it can take months, sometime years, to become fluent in the language of symbols. Be patient with yourself and, trust me, you will get there. You do not have to become skilled in reading the meanings of Hebrew letters, or adept at astrology, Tarot, guides, numerology, or any of the other practices that rely on symbols. You just need to become fluent in the language of the unconscious. This symbolism is not exclusively the domain of spiritualists and specialists; it is absolutely accessible to you.

And this is what I hope to teach you here. Learn the language and the mystery of the unconscious and apply it to your life. Bring the unconscious, the dream world, into your everyday life, and the events that compose your day-to-day existence will reveal themselves as the amazing blessings that they are. God talks to us all the time—in dreams and in waking, when we are with each other and when we are alone. We just have to wake up to hear it.

ABOUT THE AUTHOR

Doris E. Cohen, PhD, has been a clinical psychologist and psychotherapist in private practice for more than thirty years, treating thousands of clients. Her approach uses therapy, hypnotherapy, past-life regressions, and dream analysis. A certified healer, metaphysical intuitive, and communicator with Guides and Angels of the Light, Doris has given more than ten thousand medical, spiritual, and relationship readings. She has also conducted numerous workshops and has lectured nationally and internationally. She lives in Beachwood, Ohio. Visit her at *www.drdorisecohen.com.*

Hampton Roads Publishing Company

. . . for the evolving human spirit

Hampton Roads Publishing Company publishes
books on a variety of subjects, including
spirituality, health, and other related topics.

For a copy of our latest trade catalog, call (978) 465-0504
or visit our distributor's website at *www.redwheelweiser.com.*
You can also sign up for our newsletter and special
offers by going to *www.redwheelweiser.com/newsletter/.*